REVIVAL IN ROMANS

REVIVAL IN ROMANS

*An Exposition of the Epistle to the
Romans Chapters 1 through 8, with
emphasis on its evangelistic thrust.*

by
WALTER K. PRICE

ZONDERVAN PUBLISHING HOUSE
GRAND RAPIDS, MICHIGAN

DEDICATED
To My Wife

Ζωή μου, σᾶς ἀγαπῶ

PREFACE

MY UNDERSTANDING OF THE EPISTLE OF ROMANS has been influenced by writers of varied theological persuasion — from Ironside, who gave to me a love for expository preaching; to Brunner, who provided a satisfactory interpretation of Genesis 3 and its relation to the thinking of the apostle Paul. The outline of this book has been wrought out in revivals as I have preached its substance in numerous evangelistic meetings in Southern Baptist churches. Therefore, the homiletical structure can be traced throughout; however, it has been greatly revised for publication. I have purposefully preached from the epistle of Romans during revivals because it has been honored of God throughout the history of the Church as a choice instrument of the Holy Spirit in producing spiritual awakenings.

To profit most by the evangelical and devotional content of this book, it should be read alongside an open Bible — preferably the American Standard Version of 1901, which is quoted throughout, with but two exceptions.

WALTER K. PRICE

Danville, Kentucky

CONTENTS

REVIVAL IN ROMANS

1

The 'I Am' Sayings of Paul

Text: Romans 1:1-16

HISTORICALLY, THE BOOK OF ROMANS HAS BEEN THE AXIS OF many great revivals. It was when the church of the Middle Ages had stumbled to a halt in the midst of ecclesiastical intrigue that Martin Luther discovered the liberating message of this book. Here began the Protestant Reformation. The Evangelical Revival of the eighteenth century had a similar beginning. John Wesley was converted in Aldersgate Street, London, as a Moravian Christian read from Luther's *Commentary on Romans*. Our present serious return to New Testament Christianity has its roots extending back forty years to the time when the peaceful dreams of early twentieth century theologians were being shattered in the trenches of France. A young Swiss pastor, Karl Barth, discovered the dynamic message of this epistle and wrote a commentary that marked a turning point for the church that had long wandered in the barren wilderness of liberalism. It would seem that the epistle to the Romans has been elected to a special place in the plan of God for revival.

Paul's epistle to the Romans is unique and unlike anything else that we find among the 13 or 14 books that have been traditionally attributed to him. This is because he is writing to a church that he had not founded and which he had never visited. That which explains the other epistles will not explain this one. In the vast literature that is available on Romans, there are to be found scores of theories as to why he wrote this particular epistle. When all of these are gathered up, we will find that Paul's expositors are saying just three things about his purpose in writing it.

First, there is what may be called an *apologetic* aim. In the spring of 58 A.D. Paul was resting in Corinth after his third missionary journey. Following a necessary trip down to Jerusalem to deliver gifts that he had collected for the needy members of the church there, he would then turn his attention to the remote regions of the West where the Gospel had never been preached. In order that churches might be established in the chief cities of the Roman Empire's thirty provinces, someone would have to go to Spain, Gaul, and even up into Britain. This Paul proposed to do. But for this project he would need the backing of the large and influential Roman church. Since they did not know him, he must introduce himself and his message. This he did in the Roman epistle.

Then, there is what is called a *didactic* aim. Paul may have sensed that his ministry was drawing to a close. Considering the general and systematic structure of the epistle, it would represent for Paul a final statement of the leading principles of the Christian faith which he wished to deposit with an established church for safe keeping.

A third possible aim may be derived from the fact that Paul was seldom free from the attacks of the Judaizers — those Jews who followed him about the Roman Empire and subverted the churches he had established by teaching his new converts that to detach the Gospel from the law was false Christianity. These teachers also maligned Paul's personal character. As soon as his plans were known, these Judaizers would hasten to Rome also — perhaps they were there already. In this letter Paul offers to the Roman church a true statement of his teachings. Hence the epistle of Romans has a possible *polemic* aim.

Whatever his purpose may have been, it is helpful to note that some of the deepest and most profound truths of Paul's epistles come to us out of his conflicts. The open hostility of his antagonists and the desperate problems Paul often faced caused him to pen for posterity some of the most meaningful revelations to be found in the New Testament. God's method has not changed. Some of our clearest and deepest insights into the plan and purpose of God for our lives will often come to us out of our heartaches and out of the difficult situations that environment forces upon us.

The whole of this introductory section, verses 1-16, can be understood best as we note a thrice repeated affirmation which Paul makes. He says: "I am debtor," "I am ready," and "I am not ashamed." This three-fold affirmation is the secret of Paul's missionary enthusiasm.

I AM DEBTOR

In verse 14 Paul declares, "I am debtor both to the Greeks and to the Barbarians, both to the wise and to the foolish." If we will look back at what he has said in verses 1-7, we will find that this debt which he so keenly felt is based upon three things: his personal calling (verse 1); his personal Saviour (verses 2-4); and his personal responsibility (verses 5-7).

Paul sees in his own *calling* several salient facts. By that calling he is constituted "a *servant* of Jesus Christ" (verse 1). Though this word "servant," or more literally "slave," was in constant use by the ancient Semite, as it still is today among the Arabs when one refers to himself in relation to a superior, it has a much deeper significance for Paul than merely that of contemporary usage. It implies the obligation of a deep love. Here is a paradox: man by nature is free, yet by nature we are so constituted that we must also be dominated. The natural man is dominated by sin and is a slave of sin. In John 8:34 we find the same word that Paul uses here in Romans 1:1, when Jesus said, "Everyone that committeth sin is the bondservant of sin." In this use of the word Paul confirms what so many believers fail to realize — salvation does not eliminate slavery, it simply changes one's master. Though once under the dominion of sin, through salvation we are now under the dominion of Christ. Where formerly we were moved at the will of sin, we are now moved at the will of the Saviour. This Paul understood as a vital part of his calling, as should every Christian.

Another aspect of his calling is that of his *apostleship*. He says in verse 1, "Paul . . . called to be an apostle. . . ." The word means "a sent one." We find the entire Trinity involved in this calling and commission of the apostle Paul. In Galatians 1:15 he states that God called him from birth. In Acts 9:15 we find Jesus active in the call at the time of Paul's conversion. Then in Acts 13:2 we find the Holy Spirit active in calling him to specific fields of endeavor. It is no wonder that he felt this calling to be a debt that he must discharge with grave concern. Though it is an open question as to whether there are apostles after the time of the New Testament, it is no doubt true that the things that constituted Paul an apostle are still operative in the lives of believers today, for God calls and elects us to salvation, Christ saves us, and the Holy Spirit directs in specific areas of service. Hence, we should feel the same indebtedness that Paul did, for the basic elements of our calling are the same as his.

A last component of this calling which made Paul a debtor is·that he was *"separated* unto the gospel of God." The word which Paul uses comes from the same root that the word "Pharisee" comes from. Phariseeism was a protest movement against the in-roads of Hellenistic culture and its influence on Jewish life and thought. But it was a separatist movement that became an end in itself. There is a lot of contemporary fundamentalism that is no better than first-century Phariseeism. It emphasizes separation in an altogether negative sense. It is a separation "from" the world that leaves a void to be filled only with spiritual pride. Paul's emphasis was positive and thus more spiritually wholesome. He was separated "to" something — the Gospel of God. There is a vital place for the Christian doctrine of separation, but only when that separation is positive in its emphasis, leading the believer not only to separate himself from certain "worldly practices," but also leading him to a positive holiness of life in humble dependence upon the Lord.

A second prominent factor that underscores the gravity of Paul's debt to preach the Gospel is the Subject of the Gospel of God Himself. This Subject, the promised *Saviour* who is at once human and also divine, is described in verses 2-4.

There is a basic inquiry that must preface any discussion of the promised Redeemer. How are we to account for the presence of evil in our world? Is God responsible for it? Or are we to understand that there is an indissoluble dualism existing in the universe — a force of evil co-existent and co-equal with the force of good which we understand as God? Neither of these alternatives is satisfactory in the explanation of the presence of evil. If God didn't create it, and if it did not always exist, how did evil originate in our universe? It is to be accounted for through the concept of the freedom of the human will. When He originally conceived man, God endowed him with the capacity of independent and self-determining choice. He could choose to love God or choose not to love God. Ultimately man took the latter course. It is in human rebellion that evil made its advent into the world of human experience. It is this situation that calls forth the need for a Redeemer.

But this was not unanticipated by God. Therefore the coming of the Saviour was no divine afterthought. In fact, we can trace the plan of God in sending the Redeemer back through the recesses of time into eternity, for the book of the Revelation speaks of Jesus as the Lamb "slain from the foundation of the world" — i.e., slain in the mind of God. Antecedent to the creation of man, the plan of redemption had already formulated itself in the purposes of God, for God knew that man's freedom of choice would lead him into sin and hence make necessary the coming of a Redeemer. After man was created in the image of God, he did sin and was driven from the presence of God, symbolized in the expulsion from the Garden of Eden. But along with this exile came the prediction of Genesis 3:15 that the seed of woman would bruise the head of the serpent. Thus the promise of the Saviour shone through the darkness of man's sin. Each prophet in the ensuing centuries took this little gleam of light and added to it until finally it focused upon Bethlehem's barn and the realization of the coming of the Saviour of promise.

In verses 3 and 4 Paul sets forth certain facts about the person of this Saviour. He was "born of the seed of David according to the flesh," and He was "declared to be the Son of God" by the resurrection. Here is a simple statement of the humanity and divinity of Christ, and yet a concept so profound that it took the concentrated thought of the Church five hundred years to say what it means. As Son of David, the Saviour is human. The Old Testament was centuries in distilling the fact that the Messiah would be a human descendant of King David. The human identity of the Messiah begins back in the early section of Genesis. There He is described as coming from mankind — He is the "seed of woman." Then from all the races of mankind, He is to be of Shem's family. Then from all the Shemites, He will be of the seed of Abraham, and from all the nations that descended from Abraham, the Messiah will be of the nation of Israel; and of all the tribes that constitute the nation Israel, He will be of the tribe of Judah. Then of all the families in the tribe of Judah, He will be of the royal family of David.

The gospels also testify to the humanity of the Saviour. In them we find that He had a true *human body*. He was born of a human mother. He grew physically, His body being subject to the laws of physical growth as well as subject to natural instincts such as hunger and sleep. He could be weary, fearful, angry, and He could also weep. His body could be killed as well. The Saviour had a *human mind*. He was subject to the ordinary laws of mental development. He likewise had a true *human soul*, or spirit. He grew and waxed strong in spirit and was subject to temptation. The Saviour in addition had a true *human dependence* upon God. His prayer life, His faith, and His dependence upon the Holy Spirit, all testify to His true dependence upon God. His miracles were not done in the area of His divinity, but in His humanity through human dependence upon God to answer prayer (witness the resurrection of Lazarus which He preceded with two days of prayer, cf. John 11:6 and 41). Though His miracles may testify of His divinity, even more they prove His humanity!

We have so contended for the divinity of Christ against modern denials of His unique Sonship, that we have all but forgotten the profound implications of His humanity and the encouragement that a right understanding of this truth has for every believer. The point is this — though Jesus was the uniquely divine Son of God, in the Incarnation He freely divested Himself of His purely metaphysical attributes of omnipotence, omnipresence, and omniscience. Having done so, He then lived His triumphant life on earth, not through the power innate in His divine nature, but in the area of His humanity, empowered by the Holy Spirit. This seems to be the very point that Luke is making in his gospel, for he portrays Jesus as true man, living a sinless and triumphant life due to the enduement of the Holy Spirit (cf. Luke 3:21f; 4:1, 14, 18). This view does no discredit to the divine nature of Christ, for it is the only way that the Incarnation becomes meaningful. To be sure, He could have lived His earthly life in sustained perfection because He was God. But to have done so would have reflected upon His true humanity and also would have made His earthly life an impossible example to emulate.

However, when we realize that His perfect and sinless life was achieved not because of His divine nature, but through the human nature empowered by the Holy Spirit, it is then that we begin to realize the real majesty of the Incarnation. For as true man He achieved victory by utilizing the same resources of power to which every believer has access also, namely, the power of prayer, the power of the Holy Spirit, the power of the Word, the power of faith, and the power of the consecrated life.

In verse 5 we find the divinity of the Son of God set forth. Though the Old Testament is clear in its testimony concerning the humanity of the Messiah, it is debatable as to whether it clearly portrays His divinity. However, there is no doubt in the gospels and in the epistles that Jesus of Nazareth is the uniquely divine Son of God, declared to be so by the Resurrection.

Dr. E. Y. Mullins, in his book, *Why Is Christianity True?* has pointed out that the divinity of Christ can best be seen in a series of relations. For example, His relationship to sin is one of the clearest indications of His divinity. He never once confessed sin, though He condemned self-righteousness in others. His enemies could not detect sin in Him, though they watched Him carefully for just this purpose. He even challenged them, "Which of you convicteth me of sin?" He was a revealer of sin in others, for Peter cried, "Depart from me, for I am a sinful man, O Lord." He claimed to be able to forgive sin — a prerogative clearly understood to be God's alone. He even declared that His blood was necessary for the cleansing of sin in others. All of these facts exonerate Him from the control of sin and set Him apart into a realm which is other than human.

Note His relation to the law also. He contrasts Himself with other moral teachers, especially in the Sermon on the Mount, and makes Himself superior to them. He claimed to have fulfilled the law — not merely to have *kept* the law — but He was obedient to the deepest and most spiritual implications of it. He also called Himself greater than the Temple, the Sabbath, and the prophets, in Matthew 12.

In Matthew 24 and 25 we have a clear reference to His relation to providence. Here Jesus claims control over the world and is the One who will lead it to its final consummation. Consider in addition His relation to mankind itself. He was organically connected with humanity; however He is ever conscious of being separate from it. He was man, yet set Himself up as an object of faith and of worship on the part of other men. His relation to God gives salient testimony to His divinity, for He claimed a special relation to God—that of unique Son. So close was this relationship between Himself and God that He claimed to be a revealer of God in His own person. He even maintained His oneness with God at His trial, when a word to the contrary would have saved His life. We must conclude that Jesus was what He claimed to be, or else the world's most deluded impostor, worthy only of our contempt, certainly not our allegiance. But for Paul the greatest argument for His divinity was the empty tomb. For, where others have been resurrected, Jesus alone was *the* Resurrection. Thus the divine Son of God proved His divinity by demonstrating this inherent capacity for self-generation.

Throughout this introductory section we find a third factor that causes Paul to affirm, "I am debtor." It is the personal responsibility which he felt for all the world. This world-wide concern is found in verse 5, as well as in verse 14. The epistle of Romans is filled with the universal depravity of man and the universal sufficiency of the Gospel. One reason why it is so prominent in this epistle is that Paul wants to enlist the active support of the Roman church in his missionary trip to the unreached areas of the West. He perhaps felt that the cosmopolitan Romans would feel little concern for the half-barbarian people of Spain, Gaul, and Britain. Therefore he must impress upon them the debt that he feels for the spiritual welfare of these people out on the remote edge of the then known world.

I AM READY

In verse 15 Paul declares, "I am ready to preach the gospel to you that are in Rome." Paul's readiness to preach the Gospel in a general way may be due to many factors, but his readiness to preach in Rome is due to a specific spiritual preparation that he has been making for such an undertaking. This he reveals to us in verses 8-13. In these verses we find Paul's intercessory prayer for the Roman church. A close analysis of this prayer will show us the true nature of intercessory prayer, as well as the important characteristics of such praying.

In verse 8 Paul says, "I thank my God through Jesus Christ for you all. . . ." In these words are the essence of true intercessory prayer. It is prayer *to* God, *through* Christ, *for* others; i.e., it must have a proper object — God; a proper claim — Christ and His merits; and a proper motive — others. In addition to these requisites, it must be centered in a proper experience. Paul says, "I thank *my* God. . . ." He had a personal claim on the blessings of God through salvation.

Next we find some important characteristics of intercessory prayer. These are intimated in Paul's prayer in verses 9-11. First, prayer must be *definite*. This is suggested in verse 10, where Paul records a specific request requiring a specific and positive answer. When one is in the center of God's will, prayer can become very positive. The true prayer of faith is positive in believing and requesting because the faith to believe is a gift of the Holy Spirit and at the same time is a pledge of the answer. In 1540 A.D. a good friend of Martin Luther, one Fredrick Myconius, became deathly sick. Believing that he would soon die, he wrote a letter of farewell to Luther. To this letter Luther replied: "I command you in the name of God to live, because I still have need for you in the work of reforming the church. The Lord will never let me hear of your death, but will permit you to survive me. For this I am praying; this is my will, and may my will be done, because I seek only to glorify the name of God!" When Luther's letter came, Myconius had already lost the power of speech, but in a short while was well again and did not die until two months after Luther did!

Again, effective intercessory prayer is *secret* prayer. Paul in verse 9 calls God to witness the fact that he had prayed for the Roman church, suggesting that none knew of his praying save God alone. Public prayer has its important place, but the praying which gets the greatest results consistently is secret prayer. Jesus never prayed publicly except to express His thanks to the Heavenly Father for the answer to prayer offered in the secret place. His prayer life of intercession was entirely secret.

Verse 9 also gives us another fact — *persistence* is a prominent key to successful prayer. Paul says, ". . . how unceasingly I make mention of you. . . ." The eighth verse suggests the same thing because Paul literally says, "I am now thanking my God through Jesus Christ for you all." He was praying even as he wrote! Persistence is the one principle of successful praying that Jesus singled out when He gave His great model prayer in Luke 11:1-13. You see, immediate answers to prayers require no faith. If it were true that God always answers prayer immediately, then we would pray by sight and not by faith. Delay is necessary to demonstrate faith, and therefore persistence is made necessary by this delay. Immediate answers to prayer would eliminate the element of nurture and spiritual development that is inherent in every prayer situation. It is this spiritual development which is a by-product of prayer that makes prayer indispensable to the development of the spiritual life. Since time is necessary to this process, and since time infers a delay in the answer, then there must be persistence on the part of the believer until the answer comes.

Effective praying which consistently gets an answer must be grounded in a life fully dedicated to God. This truth Paul suggests in verse 9 when he speaks of serving God in his spirit in the Gospel. Luther could pray for Myconius' recovery saying, "It is my will," because his will was God's will. When we examine the nature of our requests in prayer, almost everyone could conclude that a large segment of this praying violates the injunction of James 4:1ff against praying selfishly. However, we fail to realize that one has a right to pray for personal things when his life is wholly consecrated to God, because when we are fully lost in God's will, our will becomes His, for His is ours.

In verse 10 we find that successful intercessory prayer is *surrendered* praying. Paul was not at all sure when God would answer his prayer, nor how the answer would come. One of the most illuminating spiritual lessons is to be found in the answer to Paul's prayer in these verses. We find it in the book of Acts. Paul wrote the Roman letter in the spring of 58 A.D. from Corinth. From there he went to Jerusalem, where he was arrested and taken to Caesarea. There he spent two years in prison, awaiting a trial which would probably prove fatal to him. Exercising his right as a Roman citizen, he appealed his case to the emperor. In the autumn of A.D. 60 he sailed for Rome in chains, arriving in the early months of A.D. 61. His prayer had been answered!

He began this prayer in the spring of A.D. 58. It was answered in the spring of A.D. 61. Three years delay, and yet the answer came. Mr. Moody used to observe that it took God 1500 years to answer one of the prayers in the Bible. Moses prayed for the privilege of going over the Jordan into the Promised Land. God said to him, "Speak to me no more of this matter." This was not a refusal, but a direction. Then one day, 1500 years later, we find Moses on the Mount of Transfiguration with Jesus and Elijah. He did not cross over the Jordan, as it was told him that he would not; however he did go into the Holy Land, just as he prayed that he might! God kept the prayer of Moses before Him for fifteen centuries, then He answered it!

I AM NOT ASHAMED

In a very real sense Paul's indebtedness to both Greek and Barbarian, as well as his readiness to preach the Gospel in Rome, is based on the fact recorded in verse 16, "For I am not ashamed of the gospel." This is suggested by the word "for," which links his estimate of the Gospel with his keenly felt debt, as well as with his readiness to journey to Rome.

His appraisal of the Gospel involves several facts which give us one of the finest definitions of the Gospel and its purpose that we have in the New Testament. The Gospel "is the *power* of God." The word translated "power" is a Greek word (*dunamis*) from which we get our English word "dynamite." The Gospel then is the dynamite of God. We tend to surround the cross with thoughts of self-limitation, suffering, abasement, humiliation, and shame. However, these do not comprise the dominant theme of the cross. Its dominant theme is that of power, for in the cross, and the Gospel which it made possible, we have an ultimate demonstration of God's power. In His omnipotence, God holds the universe in check, but the Gospel has made possible a higher dominion. Through the Gospel God can now dominate human personality, the highest entity we know, because it is the one thing in the universe that is most like God. The cross is a final demonstration of power and of glory, not of shame and humility, for through the Gospel of the cross God can now bring human personality back into conformity with His will without coercion, which would violate man's free will. He can do this by the persuasive power of the Gospel alone.

He further amplifies his definition of the Gospel: it is "the power of God *unto salvation.*" There is an important sense in which the Gospel has social implications. But this is secondary to the main issue, personal salvation. Since sin is essentially a personal matter — for only that which is possessed of a free will can rebel against God — so also must salvation be a personal matter. On the cross the power of God wrought out the potentiality of personal salvation for every sinner, making possible a direct encounter between the soul and God.

Again, the Gospel is "the power of God unto salvation *to everyone.*" Here is the scope of the Gospel — democratic and universal. It is democratic because its method makes it available to all. It is universal because its power is as extensive as the power of sin; hence there is none that is exempted from the blessings of the Gospel — it is for everyone.

In his fourth observation about the nature of the Gospel of which he is unashamed, Paul suggests the universality of its method, for it is "the power of God unto salvation to everyone *that believeth.*" This method of obtaining salvation is basic in the issue of eternal life because so many different "essentials" have been urged by various groups. Often people in utter confusion will say, "I don't know which is the right way of salvation. I hear so many different things. One group says that you must do good works to be saved; another says that you must be baptized; another says that you must join their particular church to find salvation; another points to the sacraments as essential elements in salvation; and others say that faith alone will bring salvation. Which is the right way?" In spite of all the confusion in answering this question, the test that points out the true way of salvation is very simple. The right way of salvation is the way that will stand the logician's test of the universal. It is the way that will work under any conceived set of circumstances. If you can envision a situation in which a person wanted to be saved but could not because of some supposed mechanical necessity, such as water to be baptized in, then that is not a Bible way of salvation.

There is but one way which will work under all circumstances and which will permit salvation irrespective of environmental conditions or restrictions. That is the way of faith. That is why Christmas Evans used to say, "I can take a man, tie him hand and foot, nail him in a barrel and then shout through a knothole what he must do to be saved, and he can do it!" The way of faith is the only universal method of salvation, for it is the only way that makes salvation accessible to all, no matter where circumstances might have thrust them. I had a professor in the philosophy department of the University of Kentucky who said one day, "The genius of Christianity lies in its method of accessibility, for it is both universal and democratic. Anyone can believe — from the president of the university to the garbage man!" No wonder Paul was unashamed, for none had to be left out when he gave the invitation.

2

The Text That Brought the World's Greatest Revival

Text: Romans 1:17

Revivals of religion have been a common occurrence in the history of the Church. When they occur, they usually have two principles in common. First, there is a key person that emerges, a man whom God particularly endows to lead in the spiritual awakening. These great revival leaders are well known — John Wesley, Charles Finney, George Whitefield, D. L. Moody, R. A. Torrey, Billy Sunday, and others. The other common factor in most great revivals is a doctrinal one. Some aspect of Biblical truth that has been long neglected in the passage of time is thrust to the forefront of Christian thought and experience.

In 1741 and 1742 the American colonies were in the midst of the Great Awakening. Its counterpart was the Evangelical Revival in England. Out of that revival came an emphasis on *the new birth* as its key doctrine. George Whitefield had such an experience on Oxford campus. John Wesley had a similar crisis in Aldersgate Street in a Moravian meeting. They arose from those experiences to infuse new life into the Church as masses on both sides of the Atlantic were swept into the kingdom of God through the new birth.

In 1801 one of the greatest revivals in American history broke out near Lexington, Kentucky. It swept up from the western part of the state to burst forth in the great camp meeting at Cane Ridge. Thousands gathered to be vitally affected by the revival's key emphasis: *the sovereignty of God and the total depravity of man.*

In 1821 a young lawyer was converted in Adams, New York. In the ensuing years God used Charles G. Finney to bring about a spiritual reawakening along the Eastern seaboard. As in other historic revivals, there was a spectacular doctrinal emphasis, this time, *the assurance of salvation.*

26

America's second Great Awakening began in 1857. From a noon prayer meeting in Fulton Street in New York City, the Spirit of God moved across the entire eastern half of the United States in the most thorough-going spiritual awakening America has ever known. Oddly enough, this revival is little known, due to the unique fact that there was no great leader to emerge along with the key doctrine, which was *the power of prayer*.

The old Moody church in Chicago had the words, "God Is Love," worked in gas jets above the pulpit. Every Moody meeting had those words painted above the platform too, for *the love and the grace of God* were the key emphases of the great Moody-Sankey revivals of the 1870's and 1880's.

Today, we may be in the tremors of another national revival. The key figure, Billy Graham, has apparently emerged. But what of the key doctrine? It may be too early to decipher; however it seems that the evangelist's words, "The Bible says," ring with more than local allusion. There is historic significance here, for *the power and the authority of the Word of God* may very well be the key doctrine of this mid-twentieth century revival.

The greatest revival in the history of the Church, however, occurred in the sixteenth century. It was in 1510 that Martin Luther found peace with God as the words of Romans 1:17 brought the liberating truth of justification by faith into his sin-fettered soul. This vital truth, long neglected by the church of the Middle Ages, became the key emphasis of the Reformation.

Thus we find profound historical significance in Paul's words, "For therein is revealed a righteousness of God from faith unto faith; as it is written, But the righteous shall live by faith," for it is this text that brought the world's greatest revival. Yet there is other than historic import here. Paul had the power to summarize doctrine and experience with singular brilliance. All of the great spiritual content of Romans is an exposition of this revealed righteousness of God — not what God *is* primarily, but what God *does* for the sinner, having sent Christ to provide an accepted righteousness for him.

A MANDATORY RIGHTEOUSNESS

Like a jewel of many facets, the righteousness of God gleams from varied angles of consideration. First, it is a mandatory righteousness. The righteousness of God demands a corresponding righteousness from man. "Be ye holy for I am holy" is the eternal decree of God. Because God is perfect, He can tolerate no imperfection nor have fellowship with man in his imperfection. This fact creates a spiritual dilemma for the sinner. Man has no power to lift himself into the sphere of God's perfection. He is already a sinner; hence he is cut off from God. But as man cannot lift himself to God, neither can God lower Himself to the sinner's level without denying His essential righteousness. Here is a spiritual impasse of separation between God and man, a gulf to be bridged only by the cross of Jesus Christ.

This demand of God's righteousness has been impressed upon us in two distinct ways—through conscience and through God's law.

There is a universality of ethical codes which testifies to the fact that all people, no matter how primitive, have an awareness of that which is right and of that which is wrong. This universal awareness we call conscience. Of course, the big problem with conscience as a guide to righteousness is that it can only tell us the *fact* of right and the *fact* of wrong. It has no power to differentiate between *what* is right and *what* is wrong. As far as the testimony of human conscience is concerned, what is right and wrong will vary from time to time and from culture to culture. So our conscience is limited. It does make us aware of the simple moral fact, but it cannot tell us what is the right thing to do. A further revelation is needed. And this we have in the revelation of the moral law of God. Conscience gives us the *fact* of morality, God's law gives us the *content* of morality.

Some have made a tragic mistake at this point in that they believe it possible to meet the righteous demands of God and thus find salvation by keeping the law through human effort. This is impossible on three counts.

Even though the righteous demands of God are revealed in conscience and more specifically in His law, we cannot be saved by keeping the law ourselves—first, because we have *a fallen nature.* Romans 8:7 says, "Because the mind of the flesh is enmity against God; for it is not subject to the law of God, neither indeed can it be." Everything within the sinner's nature moves him contrary to the law of God. To keep the law of God is to strive against the natural current of our own inclinations which surge away from God. We may make some strides in that direction occasionally, only to find ourselves inevitably encountering this spiritual resistance from within. This is the mind of the flesh opposing the law of God.

Again, we cannot be saved by keeping the law of God because of the very *nature of the law*. The law is a unity. It is so construed in the nature of things that if we violate one precept of it, we violate all of it. James 2:10 says, "For whosoever shall keep the whole law, and yet stumble in one point, he is become guilty of all." To find righteousness by the law means total obedience, not partial. It means permanent obedience, not temporary. We must keep the whole law, all our lives. If we fail just once, then the entire law is set against us, for it is a solidarity of righteous demands. Envision yourself hanging over a cliff by a chain. There are ten links in this chain. How many would have to break before you fall? All ten? Nine? Eight? No, only one is enough to send you to your death. Just so, the law is a solid chain of revealed righteousness. It is theoretically possible for a person to climb into God's favor in this way, but actually impossible, for the violation of one precept means condemnation — something everyone has already done.

Third, we cannot be saved by keeping the law of God because we are *already sinners*. We have already violated the law of God and are hence condemned. Romans 6:23 says, "The wages of sin is death." Just as one crime makes a criminal, or one murder makes a murderer, so one sin makes a sinner. We are now under condemnation because of sin that has already been committed. Even if it were conceivable that we could live a life of perfection from this moment on, there is the past which issues in our eternal condemnation. A perfect future cannot remedy a misspent past.

Here then is what we find concerning God's mandatory righteousness. It is stringent in its demands upon us. These demands are known to the sinner through conscience and through God's law. But at this point we find ourselves in a tragic state because by natural endowment, by past experience, and by the nature of the law, we are incapable of meeting God's righteous demands.

A PUNITIVE RIGHTEOUSNESS

The second demand of God's righteousness is a punitive one. Not only does the righteousness of God demand a corresponding righteousness in us, but it also demands that we be punished when we fail in this righteousness. Sin in the abstract does not exist, except in our minds. It is sin in the concrete that God condemns, and there is no sin apart from the sinner who sins. Thus sin must be punished in the sinner.

In order to understand the punitive righteousness of God, it is necessary to understand the nature of sin. However, there is no simple definition that will cover all the ramifications of sin. Perhaps we should follow the wisdom of the writer of Genesis. He does not define sin, but he portrays it and its drastic effects in the dramatic story of the Fall. Whatever one may think about the literal history of this account, it is more important that we understand the spiritual significance of the story.

Here sin is portrayed as rebellion that results in privation. Man is endowed with a self-awareness that the lower animals do not have. He is conscious of being separate and distinct in himself, and that he has the power to make decisions that will conform to the will of God or decisions which are disobedient to Him. Once aware of these facts, one has the terrible alternative of making either God or self the center of life. However, the story of Adam is the story of every person. Just as Adam rebelled against God, so have we. For each incidence of our sin is actually an act of conscious, wilful rebellion against God, in which self-will takes precedence over God's will. All sin is one — rebellion. That is why there is not only personal sin but racial sin in the thinking of Paul, as we shall see in the fifth chapter of Romans. All humanity is one in rebellion against God. Sin may vary in *degree* from person to person and from time to time, but it does not vary in *kind,* for reduced to its essential nature, sin is a revolt against the dominion, will, and purpose of God.

Sin expressed itself in rebellion, but it did not end there. Because of the righteousness of God, punishment is inevitable. This punishment is expressed in terms of privation. Man is deprived of God's fellowship due to his sin. Adam and Eve are cast out of the garden, even as sin still separates one from God.

Once outside the garden — the sphere of God's control and dominion — man is subject to all the contrary influences of evil. Cast
away from fellowship with God, human personality — created in
the image of God, given the ability to love God, know God and
choose to do God's will — is now devastated by sin. That is why
we as sinners have no capacity for God apart from regeneration.
The image of God has been distorted in us. Our volitional, rational
and emotional powers are all perverted by sin. We cannot know
God, love Him, nor choose to do His will, until the image of God
is re-created in us by the new birth. This is the privation due to
the sinner's rebellion against God.

A REVEALED RIGHTEOUSNESS

There is a third element that we must consider, one that
Paul notes especially in this text, i.e., the righteousness of God
is a revealed righteousness. It is important that we remember
that the righteousness that Paul speaks of here as being revealed
is not primarily what God *is*, but what He *does*. Granted — God
is righteous. This is an essential element of His nature. But what
Paul speaks of here is more than an attribute of God. It is a
righteousness that expresses itself in the divine activity of taking
the unrighteous sinner and providing for him that which he cannot provide for himself — an accepted righteousness which makes
fellowship with God possible. God demands righteousness. He
also provides it! Here is the great expression of God's grace. Because He is holy, He can demand no less than holiness. We are
incapable of achieving this holiness. But what we are incapable
of achieving, God in grace provides freely for us.

Paul labored throughout his ministry under the stigma of
being a religious innovator. He was hounded across the Roman
Empire by a group of religious enemies, the Judaizers, whom he
deals with pointedly in the epistle to the Galatians. As soon as
he had established a church or a new work, they moved in to
charge him with perverting the Gospel, when in reality they
were the Gospel perverters and innovators, teaching that the
legal tenets of Judaism were essential elements in the Gospel also.

To preclude this possibility here, Paul links the truth
that he is expounding in Romans with the Old Testament, in
order to show that this righteousness of God is revealed in the

Old Testament also. He quotes from Habakkuk 4:2 in which the prophet says, "Behold his soul is puffed up, it is not upright in him; but the righteous shall live by faith." The word "faith" in Habakkuk means "faithfulness." It implies a trustful self-surrender to God. The foreign conqueror prides himself in his own strength. The humble Israelite, by contrast, puts his confidence and trust in God alone. The enemy shall perish. The Israelite, who alone is righteous in God's eyes, shall live.

Of course, we must not read too much into the words of the prophet. What Habakkuk means is something different from what Paul means when he takes the passage and spiritualizes it (a liberty that Paul takes with the Old Testament several times in Romans) in order to support his point, and to make it relevant and meaningful to his readers, who were not trained in the rabbinical method of interpretation as he was. When Habakkuk uses the words, "shall live," he means deliverance from the present crisis and evil of the Chaldean invasion, and also the possession and blessing of the Promised Land. Paul sees in these words a deeper spiritual meaning as it is applied to the believer, namely, deliverance from sin's condemnation and the possession of eternal life. Just as the faithful Israelite is declared righteous, so the believing sinner is also declared righteous. Just as the faithful Israelite is delivered from the danger of the Chaldean invasion, so the sinner is delivered from the danger of his sin.

However, this righteousness of God is not seen in the Old Testament only; it is also revealed in the Gospel. It is difficult to tell exactly to what Paul refers when he says, "For therein is revealed a righteousness of God." The word "therein" may refer to the statement in verse 16, "to everyone that believeth." In that case Paul means that the righteousness of God is revealed to the eyes of faith. It is more probable that it has reference to his first statement in verse 16, "For I am not ashamed of the gospel," for in the Gospel is revealed this righteousness of God. What the Gospel does for the sinner is to bring him face to face with his own sinfulness and his bankrupt condition, and then it imparts to the sinner who responds to the Gospel message in faith, a needed righteousness that effects spiritual reconciliation and restoration.

Even if his above allusion is to the Gospel and not directly to faith mentioned in verse 16, Paul does definitely suggest faith as one of the vital elements in the revelation of the righteousness of God when he precedes his quotation from Habakkuk with the words, "from faith unto faith." The Gospel is the proclamation of the truth concerning the righteousness of God. Faith is the medium of appropriating this truth to one's own need and experience.

The precise meaning of these words, "from faith unto faith," has been variously understood. The Early Church Fathers read in them a reference to a progressive transformation from the faith of the Old Testament to that of the New. The Reformers saw these words as a progress within the heart of the individual, i.e., from a weak faith to a strong faith. Most modern interpreters, taking the literal rendering, "out of faith unto faith," understand them to mean faith from the beginning to the end. The righteousness of God becomes a part of the sinner's personal experience in the initial response of faith to the Gospel. From that point of faith's initial experience, the seed of new life grows until it has permeated and directs the whole of conscious experience — but on the same premise of faith. Faith then is both the origin and the instrument of the righteousness of God in the sinner's experience, for it is through faith that this righteous activity of God is both introduced and progressively expanded in the sinner.

A REDEMPTIVE RIGHTEOUSNESS

We come now to a fourth element in our consideration: the righteousness of God is a redemptive righteousness. In this final truth about God's righteousness, we see a paradox emerging in divine activity. The mandatory and punitive righteousness of God means that there is a gulf existing between God and sinful man. But in His revealed and redemptive righteousness, we find God closing the gulf by initiating the possibility of salvation for the sinner.

When we were discussing the demands of God's righteousness upon the sinner, we found that these demands have been revealed through human conscience and through the fuller revelation of divine law. But the law only condemns; it cannot save because of three insuperable difficulties — the fallen nature of man; the fact that man is already a sinner, thus condemned; and the fact of the solidarity of the law. If the righteous activity of God has found a way to save the sinner, it must do it by solving the problem created by these aforementioned difficulties. In fact, it is in the light of these difficulties that we can best understand the redemptive righteousness of God expressed in the saving work of Christ upon the cross.

The first difficulty in the way of salvation is the *fallen nature* of man. The sinner is by nature incapable of conforming to the law of God and thus achieving the essential righteousness expressed by the law. The fallen nature is not so much a spiritual entity transmitted from generation to generation, as it is a sinful conditioning that the entire race has fallen heir to over the aeons of human development. However, the way man came by this nature is not so much the issue as it is the dreadful fact. When one reaches an age of moral responsibility, he will inevitably rebel against God's will, expressed in His law, because of the natural endowment of this sinful conditioning. Thus by our very nature we are incapable of adhering to God's law.

The remedy for this condition lies in the experience of the new birth. The fallen nature is not eradicated in this experience, it is counteracted. A higher power — a divinely-given incentive for righteousness — is infused into the soul of the sinner in regeneration. That is why Jesus said to Nicodemus, "Except a man be born again, he cannot see the kingdom of God," i.e., he does not have the capacity to experience divine realities apart from the new birth. Immediately upon one's acceptance of Jesus Christ as personal Saviour, he is made to be a partaker of the divine nature. Where once he had no desire to keep God's law, in regeneration he is given both a desire and the potentiality of power to conform to the law of God — not in order to be saved, but because he is saved. Thus the first difficulty is solved.

The *solidarity of the law* is another problem in the way of the sinner's salvation. The law is not to be understood as merely a series of demands. It is the expression of an organic unity, so interrelated that to violate one point is to fracture the whole. The attitude that meets satisfactorily the demands of the law is not that of a sincere attempt to comply with its prohibitions and its admonitions, causing one to achieve at times, and also to fail periodically. The attitude the law demands is one of perfect adherence. That is why Paul wrote in Galatians 3:10, ". . . Cursed is everyone that continueth not in *all* things that are written in the book of the law to do them." If this perfect adherence is once failed in, then the sinner is guilty — just as guilty as if he had violated every precept in the book.

How then is man, who has violated its parts and thus the whole, saved? Listen to the words of Paul in Romans 5:19: ". . . so through the obedience of the one shall many be made righteous." That One is Christ, who lived a perfect life. He kept every precept of the law perfectly, from the first moment of moral consciousness after the Incarnation, to the last hour of life amid Golgotha's darkness. Our imperfection is transferred to Him, and His perfection is transferred to us. We stand clothed in His righteousness. When God sees the repentant sinner, He sees him swathed in the imputed perfection of Christ. Hence, the solidarity of the law is maintained and the sinner justified through the imputed righteousness of Christ. The second problem is solved.

The third difficulty in the way of salvation is the fact of *past sin*. The law of God cannot be violated with impunity. Sin must be punished. To reform now and live a perfect life in the future would not provide a solution for the sin of the past. It must be punished. Yet the Word of God is not only consistent in its testimony that sin must be punished, it is also definite in the proposition that the punishment may be inflicted upon a substitute. This was the dramatic proclamation of every smoking altar and bleating lamb from the day that Abel's offering was accepted and Cain's rejected, to the last offering on the Day of Atonement before the veil of the temple was rent, signifying the end of the Old Testament economy. Now it is in the light of this great truth that Isaiah, in his great climactic Servant Poem, speaks of the work of the Suffering Servant with these words, "But he was wounded for our transgressions, he was bruised for our iniquities; the chastisement of our peace was upon him, and with his stripes we are healed" (Isaiah 53:5). And it is in fulfillment of this great redemptive reality that Jesus climaxed His ministry by dying on the cross — the sinner's Substitute. That is why Paul says in II Corinthians 5:21, "Him who knew no sin he made to be sin (a sin offering) on our behalf; that we might become the righteousness of God in him." And with this powerful truth the third difficulty of punishment for past sin is surmounted, and the reality of the redemptive righteousness of God enters into human experience to set the sinner free.

3

Human Action and Divine Reaction

Text: Romans 1:18-32

Having presented the theme of the epistle of Romans in the previous verses, Paul begins with verse 18 to launch into the first major section of the book. In this section, covering 1:18-3:20, he will demonstrate the sinfulness of man, in order to highlight against this dark background the righteousness of God. In the epistle of Romans Paul uses the most common New Testament word for "sin" 48 times. The prominence of this subject is impressive when we realize that he uses the same word only 14 times in all of his other letters combined.

Paul will be concerned with three things in this section which is given to the sinfulness of man — the sinfulness of the Gentiles (1:18-32), the sinfulness of the Jews (2:17-3:20), and the judgment of God against both (2:1-16).

Under the general subject of the righteousness of God revealed against the background of human sin (1:18-3:20), we find Paul's first thesis in the latter half of chapter 1. It concerns itself with the sinfulness of the Gentile world. Here Paul deals with two facts which are in cause and effect relationship. First, the action of sinful man in forsaking God (verses 18-23); and then the reaction of a holy God in forsaking man (verses 24-32).

Sin is a dramatic power in human experience. Like a sickening vortex, the maelstrom of sin drags its victim ever downward. This fact is vividly set forth by Paul in these verses. He demonstrates the downward track of the pagan Gentile who could have experienced God, but who turned from the potential knowledge and experience of God to baser things. There are three steps in the devolution of the Gentile's spiritual experience.

37

REJECTED THE KNOWLEDGE OF GOD

The first thing that Paul notes is that the Gentiles rejected the knowledge of God (verses 19, 20). It is not that the pagan
never knew God; the issue is more serious than that. He knew God
and then turned from this knowledge. This is substantiated by
the paradoxical words of Paul in verse 20, "The invisible things
of him since the creation of the world are clearly seen." Invisible
things — clearly seen!

The question naturally arises in the mind of the modern
reader of these verses, can God really be known? The answer
of the agnostic is "No!" But in that positive assertion he contra-
dicts himself because he posits something about God. He describes God as unknowable, hence stating something knowable
about Him, namely, that He is unknowable! But even to those
who believe that God can be known, the problem is not a simple
one, for there emerges an apparent dilemma in the quest for the
knowledge of God. If God can be defined and described, then
He is not infinite. If He cannot be defined and described, then
He is unknowable. Conscious of this dilemma, some theologians
and philosophers have insisted that God can be known and described in only two ways.

First, there is what is called the way of *negation*. We can
describe what God is by saying what He is *not*. This method
attempts to understand God by denying to Him all of our crea-
turely and finite limitations. It is a definition of God in negative
terms. What God is, is thus inferred from what He is not. But
a negative description is never very satisfactory, for we can say
what God is not and yet know very little about Him through
these dissimilarities.

A second way is that of *analogy*. God is described by saying what He is *like*. Here we do get a positive description, but
it too is limited because it comes from our own finite experience,
and in each incidence we must say, "God is like this, only far
above this." To say that God is like, yet fundamentally different,
is confusing to say the least.

Unless there is some other way to know an infinite and
transcendent God, we are destined to frustration in the search
for this knowledge of Him. But there *is* a way of knowing Him,

because this transcendent and infinite God has chosen to *reveal* Himself to man. This is a satisfying and successful way to know God because the understanding of Him is not contingent upon our finite faculties to penetrate metaphysical realities, but upon His initiative and willingness to make Himself known to us.

This is the very point that Paul is making here in verse 19 and following. He states that the everlasting power and divinity of God can be clearly seen through the things that are made, i.e., God has revealed Himself in *nature*. From the days of Aristotle and Plato there have been certain classic arguments for the existence of God taken from the revelation of God in nature. For example, there is an argument taken from the axiom of cause and effect, called a "cosmological" argument for the existence of God. It reasons: there must be an origin, a "whence" of all existence because for every effect there must be an adequate cause. The universe is an effect; so there must be a cause greater than the effect, a greater uncaused First Cause. Thus there is posited the existence of God. Since this argument had been formulated by Greek philosophers by the time of Paul, it may be that he had this in mind when he states that God's power can be seen revealed in nature.

There is another classic argument for God's existence called the "teleological" proof. It was formulated and refined before the time of Paul by Socrates, Plato, and Philo. The thesis is simple. Nature shows order, design, and purpose. If there is design, there must be a Designer. Again we deduce the existence of God. This reasoning may lie behind Paul's statement that the divinity of God is also demonstrated in nature. It should be remembered that these arguments do not prove the existence of God. The finite can never prove the infinite. However, they do help us to understand the proposition of Paul that God has revealed Himself in nature. They also help us to understand that faith is not an irrational thing, nor is it something that we are called upon to hold in contradiction to all logic and reason.

God has also revealed Himself in *history*. There was a very great and radical difference in the way that the Greek and Roman regarded history and the way that the ancient Hebrew interpreted it. For the Hellenist, whose view was the dominant ancient classical one, history moved in a cycle within which events repeat themselves with purposeless repetition. Time had no ultimate value for the Greek because history began nowhere and ended nowhere. But for the Hebrew it was different. He saw history not as a circle, but as a straight line. For him history was a great drama whose direction was determined by the over-all purpose of God; it is an arena in which He expresses His will. It might be difficult for us to see the purpose of God when we examine any given segment of history, but when we look over the entire panorama there is clearly etched a revelation of God.

A fuller revelation of God is to be found in *Scripture*. This has been customarily called "special revelation" — opposed to general revelation of God in nature and history. However, this special revelation is built upon the foundation of general revelation because the writers of Scripture speak to those who have a belief in God. It takes for granted a belief in Him and proceeds in its revelation on that basis. The Bible is a record of God's dealing with an elect people — Israel. In His dealing with the nation He progressively reveals Himself and His purpose of redemption.

The fullest revelation of God, however, is to be found in *Jesus Christ Himself*. God is always limited by the medium through which He attempts to reveal Himself. In nature, in history, even in the written literature of the Bible, there is encountered some limitation. Since human personality is the one thing in the universe most like God, we find the fullest revelation of God in the personality of Jesus Christ. His sinlessness facilitated this revelation also, because it coupled with the human personality a sinless atmosphere in which God could work unrestrained. If personality is the one thing most like God in the universe, then sinless personality is exactly like God. So beyond Christ no fuller revelation of God is possible.

Thus God *has* revealed Himself. He has done it to some extent in nature, as Paul shows here in Romans 1. He has done it to a greater extent in history and in the Scripture, along with the fullest revelation of God that is to be found in Christ. In the light of these facts we can begin to see the extent of the Gentile's sin which Paul exposes in verses 19, 20. No wonder he concludes these verses by saying that having rejected the knowledge of God, they are without excuse.

REFUSED TO GLORIFY GOD

In verse 21 we find a second indictment against the Gentiles. Besides refusing the knowledge of God, they refused to glorify God. It is not so much that they refused to attribute glory to God — this is only a matter of lip service. But, Paul says, "Knowing God, they glorified him not as God." They refused to submit to Him and to give Him the rightful place as Lord in their lives. You may sing the praises of God and talk of the wonders of God, but you have not really glorified Him until your will, over which God has made you sovereign, is freely surrendered to the dominion of God. This is true because the human will is the only area in which God is not already sovereign. Consider it! This area of your life, the human will, is the only place in the vast universe of God in which He is not in sovereign control! He will not be universally glorified until He has conquered the last formidable stronghold of resistance. And it is over that last formidable stronghold that you alone have absolute control.

Having received the revelation of God, these pagans refused to act in accord with that revelation by yielding themselves to God. Paul labels this attitude a sin of ingratitude. Here we have a solemn truth. When God impresses man with Himself, the response that God expects is one of thankful surrender. This the Gentiles did not render. His expectation has not changed. God does not reveal Himself to you in order to satisfy your intellectual curiosity about divine realities. God reveals Himself to you in order to get the only response that will glorify Him — a grateful and thankful surrender of yourself to Him.

Now Paul notes the consequences of their refusal to glorify God. The first result is that they entered into a life of *futility*. He says, "They became vain in their reasonings." Today our English word "vain" means "proud." This is not what Paul meant, however. The word that he uses means "worthless" or "useless." It has in it the idea of something being devoid of result or success. They attempted to achieve something substantial in life after their rejection of the knowledge of God, but their quest became futile. Here is a truth many need. Some have made culture, wealth, intellectual endeavor, or society the ultimate quest of life, and sooner or later they have found the search to be futile. The reason is that they made these things, which are inherently good, an end in themselves. Theirs was the wrong frame of reference. The only way the secondary things of this world can provide happiness is when they are sought in the context of the will of God for the life of the individual.

There is a second thing that Paul states about the refusal of the Gentiles to glorify God in self-surrender; they became *desensitized spiritually*. He says of them, "And their senseless heart was darkened." When one refuses to accept the revelation of God and act upon it in self-surrender, there is the inevitable consequence of the hardened heart. The power of the sinner to respond to the call of God is progressively impaired until finally a point is reached when the sinner cannot respond. He becomes desensitized spiritually. Paul intimates that these Gentiles had already reached that point, because the word that he uses, "darkened," suggests that there was a definite point reached when the light went out in their lives. Here is the essence of the unpardonable sin elucidated in the experience of these Gentiles, for they had crossed the divine deadline.

RESORTED TO IDOLS

In verses 22 and 23 we find a third step in the course of Gentile sinfulness. Since one cannot tolerate a spiritual vacuum in the life, and having rejected the knowledge of the true God, and by refusing to glorify God by surrendering to Him, the Gentiles did the inevitable — they resorted to idols.

It is interesting that the one defection from God that is most mentioned and condemned in the Bible is idolatry. No other sin is alluded to as often as idol worship. The reason is apparent. Man is innately religious. He must worship something. As soon as God is expelled from the thought and experience of the individual, he must turn to something else. To whatever he turns as a replacement for God, it becomes an object of worship, an idol. For an idol may be anything from crude images of the pagan to the sophisticated gods of economic security, social position, or personal prestige. Time may refine the object of our worship, but the subjective fact is ever the same — the directing of our devotion to something other than God.

The sequel to this three-fold pagan defection is noted in verses 18 and 20. Against them "the wrath of God has been revealed" (verse 18). Karl Barth has noted that wrath here is the revelation of God without Christ in it, just as righteousness is the revelation of God with Christ in it (verse 17). Verse 20 gives the second sequel. They are "without excuse." Here we find what seems to be the inspired answer to the provocative question: Is one lost who never hears the Gospel of Christ? Paul's answer is not an unqualified "yes." He answers the question in another way by saying that there are none in such circumstances, for all, even the most isolated and neglected of people, have received enough of the knowledge of God, which is revealed in nature, that if they acted upon the light they are given, they would come to a saving experience with God. If they do not act upon the light they have, they too are without excuse. This becomes a terrible indictment, with a tremendous modern day implication when we realize that these pagans about whom Paul has been writing had only the revelation of God in nature. And yet this was enough to render them without excuse! If the pagan is condemned because he did not concede to the knowledge of God received in nature, how much more terrible must be the consequences of rejecting the knowledge of God in this day of full and complete revelation!

Preceding verse 24 we noted the human element in action — *man forsaking God*. In verses 24-32 we consider the divine reaction — *God forsaking man*. This inevitable divine reaction Paul declares in the thrice-repeated dirge: "God gave them up!" A. T. Robertson said of these words: "They sound to us like the clods falling on the coffin as God leaves man to work his own wicked will."[1]

The word that the apostle uses when he states that "God gave them up," means *to deliver over to the power of*. It is used of delivering one to prison, as when Saul of Tarsus dragged men and women from their homes and committed them to prison (Acts 8:3). It was also used when Jesus was bound and delivered over to Pilate for sentence (Matthew 27:2). Paul uses it with reference to the sinner whom God delivers over to the consequences of his sin. It is not to be considered as merely a permissive thing, as if

[1] A. T. Robertson, *Word Pictures in the New Testament* (Nashville, Tenn.: The Broadman Press, 1931), Vol. IV, page 330.

God in desperation permits the determined will of man to digress
from Him. It has a judicial ring in it. This is divine judgment
against those who refused the knowledge of God, who refused
to glorify God, and who resorted to idols.

When the Gentiles resorted to idols God gave them up to
idolatry (verses 24, 25). When they refused to glorify God, He
gave them up to glory in themselves and their vile passions
(verses 26, 27). When they refused the knowledge of God, God
gave them up to a depraved mind (verses 28-32). To facilitate the
understanding of this section, here are these verses in outline:

HUMAN ACTION		DIVINE REACTION
1:19, 20	cf.	1:28-32
1:21	cf.	1:26, 27
1:22, 23	cf.	1:24, 25

The clear, though inverted, relationship of these verses
must be kept in mind if we are to understand the dynamic cause
and effect relation between this human action and divine reaction.

GOD GAVE THEM UP TO IDOLATRY

Paul now unfolds this reaction of God to Gentile apostasy.
First, God gave them up to idolatry (verses 24, 25). The "wherefore" of verse 24 refers back to the two verses immediately preceding. The Gentiles "professing themselves wise. . . . became
fools and changed the glory of the incorruptible God for the likeness of an image of corruptible man, and of birds and of four-
footed beasts and creeping things." "Wherefore God gave them
up" to this idolatry.

The particular aspect of evil that is portrayed here is that
of *sin's degrading power*. Quick and inevitable the gamut was run
—from God to the worship of snakes! Paul notes three aspects
of this degrading potency of sin. He points out that it degraded
them *physically* (verse 24). The lust of their hearts to which they
were committed resulted in "uncleanness, that their bodies should
be dishonored among themselves." There is a definite sense in
which the sin of man will corrupt his physical constitution. The
Bible says, "Be sure your sin will find you out." One of the ways
that it does find the sinner out is in his external appearance. It
is true that everyone bears the mark of sin in his body in that

all are dying physically, but some more dramatically portray the bodily consequences of sin in bloated face, bleary eye, and tired gait.

Next, he shows that sin degraded them *mentally* (verse 25a), "for that they exchanged the truth of God for a lie." The Gentiles had an experimental knowledge of God, but this knowledge was not retained by them because they did not act upon it. They became so perverted in their sin that they turned to a lie. This demonstrates just how sin can degrade the rational faculties of man. This does not mean that the natural man had no power to ferret out truth in other areas. The unregenerate mind of man is still endowed with great propensities to investigate the world around him and to discover and systematize the truth concerning it. It does mean, however, that sin has so weakened the mental faculties of man that his quest for truth in spiritual realms is jeopardized. In the first incidence, if it were not for the self-disclosure of God in divine revelation, the natural man would be so lost in the morass of spiritual ignorance that he could never arrive at any satisfying spiritual enlightenment. But not only is this primary principle so, but even with the revelation of God that we have received, sin can still pervert our reasoning about revealed spiritual realities, as in the case in point.

In the last part of verse 25, the writer shows a third element in the degenerating power of sin, namely, that sin degrades *spiritually*. They "worshipped and served the creature rather than the Creator." The degrading power of sin cannot eradicate the religious tendency of man, but it does subvert it. It misdirects it from God, its true Object, to lesser things — "from the Creator to the creature," Paul says. One of the most salient testimonies to the spiritually degrading power of sin is recorded in Matthew 8:28ff. Jesus had come into the country of the Gadarenes. A demoniac met Him. Jesus was about to cure him when the demons within communicated with the Saviour saying, "Send us away into the herd of swine." Who can measure the depth of horror found in these words! These demons were probably once angels. They subsisted around the throne of God, until they were led to rebel against God. Because their action was irrevocable, they were cast away from the presence of God. They now plead to be sent into the bodies of the nearby pigs. Think of it! From the throne of God to the swill of the hog pen — so much had sin degraded them.

Here then is the first reaction of God as Paul describes it. The Gentiles resorted to idols. God gave them up to this idolatry with its dire consequences — the degraded body, the deranged mind, and the debased spirit.

GOD GAVE THEM UP TO VILE PASSIONS

The next reaction of God is set forth in verses 26, 27: God gave them up to vile passions. This is the direct result of what is attributed to the Gentiles in 1:21. There Paul says that "knowing God, they glorified him not as God." We have already pointed out that they refused this glory to God in that they did not surrender themselves to Him. The relation between these verses may not be immediately seen; it lies, however, in this simple fact: the Gentiles refused to yield to God, so God gave them up to yield to each other. They refused to glorify God, so God gave them up to glory in each other. The result was the repulsive situation that is delineated in verses 26, 27.

The particular aspect of evil that is portrayed here is that of *sin's perverting power.*

If the Gentiles had yielded to God when they received the revelation of God, they would have been lifted ever higher to new planes of living where legitimate desires would have experienced their fulfillment in the center of God's will. There they would have found satisfaction without regret or remorse. But they did not do this. Their quest for reality was perverted. They rejected the way of God, chose the way of sin and self — a way of fulfillment, yet a way plagued with regret and remorse and a panging conscience.

This perverting tendency is one of the most subtle of sin's faculties. It is an attempt to satisfy a legitimate desire in the wrong way. That is what Paul means when he says they "changed the natural use for that which is against nature" (verse 26). There is nothing wrong with the human sex urge. Man has been endowed with this particular motivation by God Himself. It becomes a sinful indulgence only when there is the attempt to satisfy this legitimate desire in the wrong way, i.e., outside the context of marriage. The fact that these Gentiles had crossed the lines of normalcy to homosexuality is just an additional witness to sin's perversion.

In the vivid pageant of the Eden story we find this unique feature of sin at work. Genesis 3:6 says that Eve saw "that the tree was good for food, and that it was a delight to the eyes, and that the tree was to be desired to make one wise," and so she partook of it in direct opposition to the expressed will of God. There are three legitimate human desires suggested here: there is the *physical* desire for food, the *aesthetic* desire for participation in beauty, and the *intellectual* desire for wisdom. There is nothing wrong with these desires. The evil lay in the attempt to satisfy them in the wrong way.

GOD GAVE THEM UP TO A REPROBATE MIND

This is the way that Paul describes the third attitude of God to the defection of the Gentiles. It is found in verses 28-32. The particular activity of the pagan that provoked this reaction of God is mentioned in verses 19, 20 — "That which is known of God is manifest unto them. . . ." Though they received this revelation, they refused God a place in their lives. The result: "God gave them up unto a reprobate mind." The mental condition to which God released them is described in Williams' translation as "minds that God did not approve," or "base minds" in the RSV. The word that Paul chooses to use here comes from a word which means *to test* or *to approve after testing.* Added to this is a negative factor which makes it mean "to reject after testing." God tested them to find some point of contact and potential fellowship based upon the revelation of Himself, which was designed to bring them into this fellowship. He found no response of surrender to His will because they chose to reject His revelation. God then gives them over to this state of rejection, degradation, and perversion — which is essentially what the depraved mind is.

There are several facts about the depraved mind that are expounded by the apostle.

All that Paul enumerates in verses 29-31 comprises the *issue* of the depraved mind. All of these are derived from the fountainhead of depravity. This underscores the basic fact that man is not a sinner because he sins. He sins because he is a sinner. The problem is more basic than one of overt acts of sin.

The incidences of sin are merely an indication of a radical disorder inherent in the sinner's very nature, for behind every specific act of sin there is the depraved mind that motivates the sinner to sin.

Note also the *character* of the depraved mind. Paul alludes to two characteristics of it. First, the sinner continues in spite of the fact that he has some knowledge of the inexorable workings of moral law. He knows that he cannot sin with impunity, yet he does so, as Paul expresses it in verse 32, "Who knowing the ordinance of God, that they that practice such things are worthy of death. . . ." If the sinner would but listen, he would find the universe of law and order consistent in its warning that violation cannot be without consequences. Witness the testimony of natural law. The law of gravity cannot be violated with impunity. You step out of the window of a tall building and you will be broken on the pavement below. Witness the testimony of civil law. If it were not for swift retribution for the infraction of civil law, there would soon be chaos. The fact of punishment is necessary for the very existence of civil law. Equally true is the sure punishment that will come when the ordinances of God are violated. It is not so much that the sinner is not aware of this. Paul says that he is. But because of his depraved mind, he willfully ignores it — to his own destruction.

The other characteristic of the depraved mind is its *excuses*, found in the last part of verse 32. Those who indulge in sin, even though they know the consequences of it, "not only do the same, but also consent with them that practice them." They sin themselves and are encouraged in the fact that others do likewise. There is a certain false security to be found in social sanction. Because of this fact, there is many a sin committed in the name of the social graces for which the individual feels no rebuff. A sinner in isolation may be caused to fear, but when the whole environment in which he lives is so engaged in the blatant violation of the ordinances of God, he is encouraged; thus he endorses it for his own security.

Out of Paul's discussion of human action in the process of sin and the inevitable divine reaction, come some inferences which will shed light on the meaning of judgment, grace, the unpardonable sin, the atonement, and the meaning of hell.

Judgment is described, not as some arbitrary trial-and-sentence judicial proceeding, relegated to an eschatological future (though the Bible indicates that there will be such a judgment) but to something that is going on even now in the experience of the sinner. This is a truth that the Hebrew prophets tried to impart to Israel in their teaching concerning the Day of the Lord. Granted, it is something that will climax the future in God's dealing with sinful man, but in a very real sense the Day of the Lord is an ever-present factor in the sinner's experience, for though God will judge in the future, He is also judging now. This salient fact is contained in the apostle's indictment — "God gave them up."

These words also shed light on other truths in God's dealing with the sinner. Here, for example, is light on the meaning of *grace*. In the theology of the Reformers there came into accepted use a differentiation between special grace — God's work of grace that saves the sinner; and general grace — God's work in creating certain gracious conditions conducive to man's spiritual betterment, but which do not necessarily save him. The work of God in restraining the absolute and devastating power of sin is one such condition. If it were not for this grace of God which withholds the power of sin, we would be caught up in sin's relentless current and swept unrestrained into a lost eternity. But for now, He restrains this potent force to give us space in which to repent. This is a temporary condition, however. For if we reject the opportunity that God in grace has given us, as the pagan did in the first chapter of Romans, this epitaph will be the hallmark of our experience — "God gave them up."

Here, too, is some light on the *unpardonable sin*. The words "God gave them up" are filled with finality. These Gentiles in Romans 1 had reached a point in their experience in which God's action in giving them up was irrevocable. When the sinner persistently resists the grace of God calling him to salvation, the call of grace grows weaker, and the progressive grip of sin grows stronger. This is not a reflection on the grace of God; it is inherent in the very nature of spiritual things. When the act of rejection by the sinner is participated in over an extended period of time, the ever-present call of God will inevitably become unheard and unheeded by the sinner. When this point is reached, there is a divine ratification of the sinner's determination to reject the call of God. We see this portrayed in the experience of Pharaoh. He first hardened his own heart — *human action*. Then the Bible says God hardened his heart — *divine reaction*. Jesus seems to have done the same thing when He ratified the determined will of Judas in rejecting Him. He said, "What thou doest, do quickly" (John 15:27). It is in this sense that the apostle refers to the Gentiles when he states that "God gave them up." He could no longer deal with them, not because He had no desire to do so, but because they were completely incapable of being dealt with.

Here is also some light on the complex meaning of the *atonement*. Sin carries with it the seeds of its own destruction. To judge the sinner, God need not extend a punitive hand; He needs only withdraw the hand of restraining grace. The result is judgment. When Jesus cried, "My God, my God, why hast thou forsaken me?" He suggested the withdrawn presence of God, thus judgment, for Christ had truly entered the province of sin on our behalf. P. T. Forsyth made this same observation years ago, "We are to understand the suffering of Christ," he said, "in terms of His entering the domain of sin and thus the natural consequences of sin fell upon Him. He did not take the punishment, He took the penalty."[2] This does not explain the full meaning of the atonement, however. But it is suggestive in letting us see that there are certain consequences of sin that are inevitable in the very nature of things. These natural consequences comprise at least a part of the meaning of the suffering of Christ upon the cross.

Again, here is suggested a meaning of *hell*. Whatever else hell may be, it must be understood as an extension of the condition these pagans found themselves in "when God gave them up," for Paul suggests that this action is permanent and final by the particular word that he uses. They were given over to the irrevocable influences and power of sin in this life. Since there is nothing about death which will terminate the course that man has set for himself in this life, hell must be understood as a continuation of this condition of final and irreversible separation from God, especially if we think of hell as being primarily a condition and only secondarily a place. But it is more than mere

[2]P. T. Forsyth, *The Work of Christ* (London: Hodder and Stoughton, n.d.), page 146.

separation. It is abandonment to sin's dread control, beginning in this life and continuing forever. One other notation — and we speak it with a sense of awesome dread — God is not fettered with our concepts of time and space. His dealing with the soul of man is eternal, not temporal or spatial. When spiritual conditions so arrange themselves that God can no longer deal with a person, this abandonment has eternal weight, not merely temporal. Today, there are also those whom God has given up because they have sinned away the possibility of responding to Him. Their physical bodies are still animated with natural life, but in a very real sense their souls are even now in hell.

4

THE POETRY OF THE DAMNED

Text: Romans 2:1-16

THE TEMPER OF PAUL'S THEOLOGY WAS DERIVED FROM THREE
sources, according to William Barclay: the background out of which
he came, the environment in which he worked, and the message
that he preached. He was nurtured in the intensely ethical atmosphere of Judaism. A vigorously ethical religion will inevitably in-
volve a standard of judgment, for when a carefully defined way
of life is laid down, failure to comply with its demands will have
serious consequences. With this heritage, Paul faced a Gentile
world that was notoriously immoral. No message would have availed
there which did not have a stern demand, involving the consequences of judgment also. The third thing that tempered his
religious thinking with judgment was the message that he had
received and that he preached. It was a way of life. Grace and
justification were great gifts, made possible by the righteousness
of God, but they carried with them great responsibility also. After
the Christian life is initiated in grace and justification, fruit must
follow. If this fruit does not materialize, then judgment is inevitable.

It is of little wonder then that principles of judgment soon
emerge in the epistle of Romans.

There is a problem beginning with chapter 2 concerning
the subjects of his discussion. To whom does he refer in verses
1-16? Prior to this section he has been dealing with the fact of
Gentile sinfulness. By the time we get to verse 17, he definitely
has the Jew in view. But what about these first 16 verses — is he
still addressing himself to the Gentile, or is his subject the Jew,
or both? A categorical answer to this question is impossible. Perhaps this section represents a transition in the indictment from
Gentile sinfulness to that of the Jew — a transition in which he
looks back to what has already been established, and forward to

what shall be said, and in which he expounds a judgment that will be the destiny of both Jew and Gentile. This we find clearly stated in the key verse of this transitional section: ". . . for there is no respect of persons with God. For as many as have sinned without the law shall also perish without the law; and as many as have sinned under the law shall be judged by the law; for not the hearers of the law are justified before God, but the doers of the law shall be justified . . . in the day when God shall judge the secrets of men according to my gospel by Jesus Christ" (2: 11-13, 16).

The question concerning whom Paul has in mind is not nearly so important, however, as it is to understand that this section is not primarily one of persons, but of principles. Beyond any local reference, beyond any group identification, there is to be seen in Paul's words the universal principles by which all men shall be judged. We may never be able to decide whether Jew or Gentile is the subject of verses 1-16, but we can be certain about the universal principles that arise from Paul's words. It is this fact that will provide the key to solving the difficulty that has taxed expositors from the beginning. For if this is not the case, then Paul lays himself open to the charge of contradiction when he later states that justification is by faith and not the result of works, which a superficial reading of these verses would infer. In verses 1-16 Paul seeks to establish the *absolute fact* of right and wrong, and the *absolute fact* of reward and punishment. No question arises at this time about how righteousness is obtained, for that is not yet his purpose. It was John Wesley's instruction to his preachers that with all possible energy, in order to search the conscience to its depths, that they preach the absolute law of holiness, and then and not until then, preach the hope of the Gospel. Intentionally or not, his directions follow the wisdom of Paul here in this section of Romans, for he too must convince his readers of the hopeless condition of all the human race, both Jew and Gentile, in the light of the categorical demands of God. This he does by setting forth some unalterable absolutes: sin will be punished, good works will be rewarded. Of course, he will qualify this principle later in the epistle by showing that the only good works that the sinner can do are those initiated by the work of Christ upon the cross, and which are imputed to the sinner through faith.

THE CHARACTER OF THE JUDGE

In our current text we will find two leading ideas, namely, the character of the *judged* and the character of the *judgment,* along with a suggestion which forms an undercurrent throughout this section, and which is expressly stated in verse 16, namely, the character of the *Judge.* Although the ultimate force behind the judgment is God, the Bible is consistent in identifying the Judge as Christ Himself. This Paul clearly states in II Timothy 4:1. He says, ". . . Jesus Christ who shall judge the living and the dead. . . ." In his famous sermon on Mars Hill, Paul also declares this truth when he said, God "hath appointed a day in which he will judge the world in righteousness by the man whom he hath ordained" (Acts 17:31), and then appends to this fact a vital proof — the Resurrection. For it was the resurrection that authenticated every assertion that the Saviour made. Jesus stated in John 5:27, ". . . and he (God) gave him authority to execute judgment because he is the son of man." God vindicated this claim in the Resurrection. This idea of resurrection substantiating the fact of judgment was basic to the first century preaching of the apostles, as C. H. Dodd has pointed out. That is why Paul says in verse 16 that the judgeship of Jesus is "according to my gospel," i.e., because the Resurrection was an indispensable part of the Gospel he preached (cf. I Corinthians 15:1ff).

Thus it is inevitable that the sinner face the issue of his relationship with Christ, for if he does not face Him and accept Him today as Saviour, then some day, when the gates of grace are closed, the sinner must face Him as Judge.

THE CHARACTER OF THE JUDGED

Verses 6-10 are among the most problematic in Romans, for on the surface it sounds as if Paul were saying the sinner is justified by works. We have already pointed out that he is dealing here with broad principles of absolute right which will be rewarded and absolute wrong which will be punished. In addition to this, it will be helpful for us to see that verses 7-10 are poetry. They contain four metrical stanzas of three lines each arranged in antithetical parallel. The first and last stanzas, verses 7 and 10, describe the righteous. The two middle stanzas, verses 8 and 9, describe the unrighteous. The rhyme scheme is A (verse 7), B (verse 8), B (verse 9), A (verse 10). Since poetry is never to be pressed with absolute literalness of detail, we must realize that Paul is stressing principles of right and wrong, reward and punishment, and that he is not saying that man will be justified in the judgment and given eternal life on the basis of good works.

In verse 6 Paul prefaces the poetry of this section with a quotation from the Septuagint of Proverbs 24:12 — God will render to every man according to his works. With this quotation as his thesis, he then describes the character of the righteous and the consequences of their righteousness, along with the character of the unrighteous and the consequences of unrighteousness.

Verse 7 characterizes the righteous by their "patience in well doing." The word that Paul uses — also used by Jesus in Luke 8:15 where He said that whosoever failed the test of endurance proves himself to have no root of righteousness — is made up of two words. The one means "under," the other, "to abide." The idea is that of abiding under some discipline which demands the surrender of the will to that against which one would naturally rebel. The natural man is fundamentally a rebel against God. Salvation brings the sinner into subjection to the will of God. The continuation of this subjection is the proof that a spiritual transformation has taken place. The idea is not that one is saved by remaining faithful; one remains faithful because he is saved. Steadfastness is the *result* of salvation, not the cause of it. Thus the security of the believer is an inevitable part of salvation because remaining faithful is inherent in the very experience itself. If one is saved, he will remain faithful, or "persist in well doing" as Paul puts it here.

The same idea is found in the word "seek," because in the word Paul chooses, he is literally saying "they persistently seek." The righteous then are characterized by their attitude. The emphasis is not so much on what they seek but on the attitude in which they seek "for glory and honor and incorruption, eternal life." It has to do with the disposition of their will which is consistently dedicated to well-doing. Of course, salvation in Christ alone can so radically redirect the human will which has been subverted by sin, as to make this consistency in seeking the things of God a reality. But to suggest this here would cause Paul to anticipate himself concerning the full meaning of the Gospel which he is later to unfold in Romans.

In verse 10, which is the parallel of verse 7, we find the consequences of this dedicated quest. Here the righteous are pictured as having achieved "glory and honor and peace." These things are not a reward of steadfastness, but are simply a part of the same over-all spiritual experience of which steadfastness is also a part. If and when one is right with God, inherent in this rightness is also the capacity for steadfastness and the prospect of ultimate "glory and honor and peace." One follows the other because all are latent in the experience. This Paul states in Romans 8:29, 30.

Injected between the two verses that describe the righteous, we find Paul's description of the unrighteous (verses 8, 9). This is parallelism, one of the most distinguishing characteristics of Hebrew poetry. It is a rhythm of meaning rather than of form. By employing this method, Paul causes the character and consequences of unrighteousness to stand out in studied relief against the contrasted character and consequences of righteousness. There are two things that Paul notes about the character of the unrighteous. First, theirs is an attitude of self-seeking. Paul says (verse 8) that the unrighteous are "contentious" (King James), or "factious" (ASV). It is generally agreed by critical scholars that this word is translated from the wrong root. It is from a word that means "hireling," not from a word that means "strife." It means *to act or behave as a hireling*. It is used of officeholders who seek their own gain. Hence the unrighteous are self-seeking. All sins can be reduced to one — rebellion — but behind every incidence of rebellion there is self. For the motive of rebellion is the usurpation of the self-will above God's will. Theirs was an attitude of persistent self-assertion in contrast to the persistent self-renunciation to the will of God on the part of the righteous.

The other notation that Paul makes about the character of the unrighteous is that they "obey not the truth, but obey unrighteousness." This is the logical consequence of making self the ultimate aim in life. Because man by nature is a sinner, to placate self is to obey sin, which is actually the dynamism of the self-life. This is what Paul means by the words, they "obey unrighteousness."

So awesome is the condemnation of the unrighteous that Paul resorts to four different terms to describe it (verses 8b, 9), for "wrath and indignation, tribulation and anguish" shall be their lot. This is a spiritual condition that Paul alludes to, because these things are directed against "every soul of man that worketh evil." The crude literalism that has been used to describe the destiny of the wicked in by-gone days has caused the modern mind to disregard the fact of eternal punishment altogether. Listen to one Jedediah Burchard, a Presbyterian evangelist, describing the meaning of hell to an audience in Rochester, N. Y., in the 1830's: "Do you know what hell is? I'll tell you. It's an ocean of liquid burning brimstone, that is daily replenished. It is walled in by great walls guarded by devils armed with pitchforks. High on the crest of the waves of fire the damned soul is swept toward this wall, where the sinner thinks he may find at least temporary rest, but when at last he manages to climb part way out of this sea of fire he suddenly finds himself pitchforked back and swept out by the receding tide."[3] It is this sort of thing, sincerely put no doubt, but which has nevertheless made eternal punishment questionable to the modern mind.

However, it is not right to reject the truth because of a faulty illustration. The problem is one of semantics. Jesus described eternal punishment, or hell, primarily in terms of fire. Is He to be taken literally, or are we to understand Him to mean that hell's awfulness is so intense that it defies human language to adequately convey its meaning; thus symbol must be used to help us understand what is eternal retribution? The reality of hell should be understood not in terms of physical suffering in a literal fire, but in terms of spiritual anguish — as Paul puts it here in Romans 2:8, 9.

There are several good reasons for doubting that Jesus meant that hell's punishment consists of physical suffering in literal fire. For example, the figure of fire conflicts with another figure that Jesus often used, that of outer darkness. Both cannot be literal, for they are mutually exclusive. Where there is fire there is light, not darkness. If both cannot be literal, it is better to conceive of both as figurative. Again, the imagery of fire is used

[3] Jedediah Burchard, *Sermons, Addresses and Exhortations* (Burlington, Vt., 1836).

in connection with the rich man in Jesus' parable of Lazarus. He was a disembodied spirit, for Jesus said when he died he was buried. His body was in the cemetery, his soul was in hades. On a disembodied spirit physical fire would have no effect. Again, hell is prepared for the devil and his angels, who are disembodied spirits and to whom fire, in a literal sense, would have no terror. Again, literal fire would destroy a body cast into it. But someone says, "This is not the kind of fire we are used to"; however, to say *that* is to say it is not literal fire, but something else; for literal fire as we know it would destroy a body. But what is more important, physical fire would not adapt the punishment to the sin. Sin is spiritual, not physical. To adequately make the punishment commensurate with the sin, the punishment must be spiritual, not physical. But we must remember that to question the mode of punishment is not to question the fact. The Word of God is plain in its testimony that the unsaved will find their place in eternal separation from God — a condition which Paul defines as "wrath, indignation, tribulation and anguish."

THE CHARACTER OF THE JUDGMENT

The poem which is embodied in this text seems to be the focal point of Paul's discussion concerning judgment. All that precedes and all that follows has led up to, and trails away from, the principles expounded in verses 6-10. However, we find in the material that precedes and follows these verses abundant light on the character of judgment itself. In particular there is one salient fact that stands out about the nature of the judgment, namely, its all-inclusiveness.

All time and *all people* are included in the scope of the judgment. Thus, it is a comprehensive judgment. In verse 5 the eschatological, or future, aspect of the judgment is set forth in these words, ". . . treasurest up for thyself wrath in the day of wrath and revelation of the righteous judgment of God." However, in this verse Paul also refers to a present aspect of the judgment of God. It is not only a future event, it is also going on now. It looms like a specter on the horizon of the future, but it also pervades the present, for in a very real sense, sin is being judged now. That is why Paul said in this verse, ". . . after thy hardness and impenitent heart treasurest up for thyself wrath. . . ." In the words "hardness" and "impenitent" we find a cause-and-effect relationship. This reveals a present judgment against sin, for inherent in the very nature of spiritual realities is this fact that the hardened heart follows swiftly upon the heels of an impenitent heart. An impenitent heart inevitably becomes a hardened heart, part of a divine judgment going on in this life. The self-righteousness of the Pharisees had so impaired their capacity to repent that Jesus said they had committed the unpardonable sin. Their impenitent heart had brought them a heart which was hardened to divine impressions and thus incapable of responding to them.

The word "hardened" means *dried* or *stiff*. It is a hardness or stiffness that will not bend. The figure is not that of the hardness of a rock, but that of a dried branch that is dead. Once the branch might have been supple with life and susceptible to the influences of nature, but through the process of time it has become hard, dried, and brittle. So it is with the impenitent heart. For the same result occurs here. When the sinner refuses to repent of his sin, he progressively loses the capacity to repent, as his heart becomes hardened to spiritual things. This Paul subtilely suggests as a part of the present judgment of God against sin. Yet a present judgment that is inseparably linked with the future, for impenitence brings hardness of heart, and the harder the heart becomes, the more wrath is treasured up for the day of judgment in the future.

That brings us to a second time-factor in Paul's consideration of the comprehensiveness of the judgment. Not only is it a present reality, it is also a future event in human experience. In verse 12 Paul uses words that take us into the future when all time is done and completed human experience is to be weighed in the balances — "For as many as have sinned without the law shall also perish without the law: and as many as have sinned under the law shall be judged by the law." The word "sinned" suggests an action that is completed in past time. By this construction, Paul transports us to the point of time in the future when the result of human life appears as a completed fact — the time of the end.

From this discussion of the two-fold time aspect of the judgment, it is important that we realize that the judgment of God against human sin is not an arbitrary judicial proceeding at the end of time only. Rather it is a dynamic thing that is going on even now in the sinner's experience and that will extend itself into the future, culminating in the last judgment, when the final decree of the sinner's doom is pronounced. The judgment is comprehensive, for not only is the sinner to be judged, he is being judged even now by the irrevocable cause and effect relationship of sin, impenitence, and the resulting hardened heart.

But not only is all time comprehended in the judgment; in verses 1-3 and 11-15, we find that all people are included in its scope also. None shall escape, for "there is no respect of persons with God" (verse 11). First, the Jew who had much religious privilege will be included, for Paul says in verse 12b, "As many as have sinned under the law shall be judged by the law." The Jews felt that their religious privilege would exclude them from the responsibility of answering to God for their conduct. It is against this attitude that Paul's opening remarks in this chapter are directed (verses 1-3), when he indicts the Jew for judging others when he himself is guilty of the same sins, showing that the Jew is open to self-incrimination.

This Jewish feeling of priority in God's favor was based on several factors. They were of the seed of Abraham, they were circumcised, and the rabbis had said that "circumcision is equivalent to all the commandments of the law"; they were Israelites, and the rabbis had taught that "all Israel has a part in the world to come"; and they were employed in hearing and studying the law, a virtue in itself. It is against this last confidence that James 1:22ff is directed, while the others are dealt with in Matthew 3:8ff, Romans 2:25ff, and Romans 2:17 respectively.

Note that Paul uses different words which are significant in showing that rather than being in a place of privilege because they had the law, the Jew was in a more precarious plight; for the Gentile "shall perish," but the Jew "shall be judged" (verse 12). Only the Jew is to be judged in the strictest sense of the word, i.e., by a code. The Gentile will suffer, but by the natural process of sin's consequences, while the Jew will be judged in the strict legal sense.

However, the Gentile is not excluded from the judgment on grounds of religious underprivilege. Paul says they will be subjects of the judgment because the substance of the law is "written in their hearts" (verse 15). To this fact the human conscience bears witness. We must not confuse the issue. The Gentiles will not be judged for violating conscience, but for violating the "work" or substance of the law, which Paul says the Gentile is innately aware of, or in his words, "for when the Gentiles that have not the law do by nature the things of the law . . ." etc. Man has the ability to detach himself from himself and objectively view his own character and conduct. He is thus able to act as a witness against himself. This is the function of conscience. It is not so much a positive guide to right as it is a negative witness to failure —failure to comply with the substance of the law which Paul says is woven into every human heart (verses 14, 15). The apostle seems to be saying that the Gentile will be judged by the substance, or the spirit, of the law; while the Jew will be judged by the letter of the law. Hence neither Jew nor Gentile will be excused.

It would be improper to close this discussion of the absoluteness of the judgment without noting that this judgment is delayed. Why? For one reason—that the sinner might have an opportunity to repent and be saved (verse 4). Behind the delay is the "riches of God's goodness and forbearance and long-suffering," all designed to persuade the sinner to repent and thus escape the judgment.

5

Religious But Lost

Text: Romans 2:17 - 3:8

THE JEWS OF THE FIRST CENTURY HAD MADE A MISTAKE THAT many people are still making. They confused religion and salvation. They failed to realize that there is a fundamental difference between the two — so fundamental that one can be religious and yet be lost. This radical difference can be seen in the *origin* of the two terms. Religion is human in origin, salvation is divine. To be sure, behind the "Jew's religion," a term that the fourth gospel uses almost in derision, was the revelation of God, but they had appended so much sacerdotalism to it that the divine revelation had gotten lost in man-made tradition. Religion and salvation also differ in *perspective*. Religion begins with man and attempts to reach out to God; salvation begins with God and reaches down to man. Again, they differ in their basic *philosophy*, for religion fails to recognize human depravity and spiritual incapacity, while salvation makes these facts pivotal in its work of transformation. They differ in their *content*, for religion is grounded in a system, while salvation is founded on a Person. Religion accepts and propagates a system of truth; salvation accepts the Person of Truth. They also are different in their *intention*. Religion makes man acceptable to himself, for man is the measure. Salvation makes man acceptable to God. In addition, their *dynamic* is different because religion depends on human idealism for its motivation, while salvation depends upon the transforming power of God. Lastly, they differ as to their *tense*, for religion is in terms of "do," while salvation is always in terms of "done!" Religion says, "Do and live"; salvation says the reverse — "Live and do."

The Jews were very religious, but very much lost. It is to expound this fact that Paul now turns pointedly to the Jew as he attempts to show that they are equally sinful with the Gentile and are destined for the judgment of God. This will be his thesis in 2:17 through 3:8.

INADEQUACY OF THE JEW'S RELIGION

The contemporary drift of Judaism during the lifetime of Jesus and Paul had focused upon three things in particular as sufficient grounds for religious hope. These were the Jew's covenant relation with God; their superior religious knowledge, exemplified by the fact that they were possessors of the law; and circumcision. These things Paul takes up in turn and demonstrates their inadequacy, 2:17-29.

In verses 17, 18, we find the *insufficiency of the covenant relationship*. From the divine covenant that had been made with Israel, the Jews assumed several things to be their exclusive possession. First, there was a name. Paul says, "Thou bearest the name of a Jew" (verse 17). In its etymology the name "Jew" is a title of honor. It means "praised." It was also a designation for the elect people of God. The Jews had woefully failed to realize the significance of their election, however. They had been elected to bear the message of God to the non-elect. They made this privileged position an end in itself, and they gloried in the fact that they had been chosen of God, but failed to realize why they were chosen. This classic example of election, to wit, Israel was elected to take the message of God to the non-elect, may help us understand the purpose of Christian election. It is not an end-in-itself to be gloried in. It is functional. The believer is elected to bear witness to a sinful and needy world. Thus our election has more to do with others than with ourselves.

Of great comfort to the Jews also was the fact that they had in their exclusive possession the law of God. It never occurred to them that God's intention was for Israel to be a steward of the knowledge of God, proclaiming it to others. The Jew gloried in the fact that the law was exclusively his. This is why Paul says in verse 17, the Jew "restest upon the law." The word "restest" has in it the idea of *to lean upon*. "It suggests a blind and mechanical reliance upon the Mosaic institution,"[4] says A. T. Robertson. But they went further. They not only rested in the fact that they possessed the law, they also felt that they owned

[4] *Op. cit.*, p. 338.

God! They "gloried in God" because He was their exclusive possession. Paul does not mean that they gave glory to God. The glory went to themselves because they had God as their private property. This seems to be a prevalent tendency, even among Christians, for it has often occurred in the history of the Church that when God has greatly used a group of people, or a denomination, there soon emerges this attitude of having a corner on God. When this happens, God must cease to use that particular group in a unique way, and turn to another. In W. O. Carver's *Unpublished Notes* he recalls a comment that Dr. Whitsitt made in the late 1890's that is even more germane to the issue today. "Brethren," he said, "the Lord is always going to look after the plain people. The Episcopalians were eminently respectable; and the Lord raised up the Methodists and the Baptists to look after the common people. And now, brethren, the Methodists and Baptists are getting to be eminently respectable; look out for the Salvation Army!"[5]

More than five centuries before Paul wrote these words, God had warned Israel through Jeremiah and Ezekiel that the old covenant was insufficient and was destined to be replaced by a new covenant — one in which the fundamental defect of the old covenant would be remedied. The old covenant failed because it could import neither the desire nor the power to keep God's law. In 31:31-34, Jeremiah promises a new covenant which would be superior to the old because it would derive its dynamic from the new heart (personal regeneration). This new covenant was achieved in Christ, and was then being offered to Israel, but Paul concedes that they were continuing in their blind reliance upon the old.

The second inadequacy was that of their *superior religious knowledge* (verses 19-24). Just as the Jew felt indestructible in his national life prior to the Exile, because the temple of the Lord was situated in Jerusalem, so the Jew of Paul's day felt secure because he possessed the truth of God. He saw virtue in the mere possession of this truth, whether it had any effect on his life or not. He had fallen into an altogether too common error, that of regarding truth as an intellectual quality only. God's truth

[5] Wm. Mueller, *A History of the Southern Baptist Theological Seminary* (Nashville, Tenn.: Broadman Press, 1959), page 151.

is never speculative. It is to be acted upon, for morality is a basic ingredient in any spiritual truth. The personality of man has at least three components: *intellect, emotion,* and *volition.* Truth has as its objective the *will,* but in order to move the will, the *mind* must be instructed and the *emotions* stirred to some extent. The Jews may have had their minds instructed and their emotions stirred by religious feelings, but the process was incomplete because their will was unaffected, and their lives were thus unchanged by the truth they possessed. *Knowing* and *feeling* it to be wrong to steal, or to commit adultery, or to commit sacrilege, the Jew still *willed* to do these things (verses 21-23). Due to this the Name of God was being "blasphemed among the Gentiles," as it was in the days of Isaiah (verse 24). Paul uses the quotation from Isaiah 52:5 because the name of *Yahweh* was being blasphemed when Israel was ruled over by the Assyrians. Here Paul spiritualizes the quotation—a liberty that he often takes with the Old Testament, showing that the Jews of his day are ruled over by self-will instead of God's will and truth. The result is the same—"God's name is blasphemed."

Whatever fails to move the *will* to dedicated action is of little value in the spiritual life. Because our personalities are made up partly of *emotion,* a heart-felt religion is not to be disparaged. But if religious experience stirs the emotion only and does nothing else, it is of little value. Because our personalities are made up partly of *intellect,* there must be intellectual content and doctrinal expression in our religious experience. But when man's religion is wholly in terms of intellectual quality, it is of little value. To be completely satisfying and life changing, our spiritual experience must have something of the *emotional* as well as something of the *intellectual,* but these in turn must motivate the *will,* which will then direct the life in accord with these spiritual realities. Thus it is the will that is the citadel to be stormed by the Gospel. However, in order to move the will, the mind must be informed and the emotions stirred. These in turn will generate action in the will.

The Jews believed circumcision to be essential to securing eternal life. This is obvious from the writings of the rabbis. For example, one had said, "Abraham sits before the door of hell and does not allow any circumcised Israelite to enter there" (quoted by Charles Hodge, *The Epistle to the Romans*). It is this tendency to subvert the spiritual meaning of circumcision, and to make of it a mechanical rite for obtaining salvation, that Paul indites as he shows the third insufficiency of the Jew's religion, i.e., the *inadequacy of circumcision* (verses 25-27).

Circumcision was first given to Abraham, who was justified by faith. It did not provide justification for him. He was justified first, then declared to be so through circumcision. The circumcision was given by divine direction as a seal of the righteousness that was already his (cf. Romans 4:11). The Jews of Paul's day had subverted the spiritual intent of circumcision by making of it a mechanical rite which they assumed to be necessary in the experience of salvation. There is a prevalent human tendency to emphasize the external at the expense of the deeper spiritual meaning of any given ceremony. We see it expressing itself today when people fail to understand the meaning of baptism as symbolic of a deeper spiritual reality, and make of it a mechanical rite for the washing away of sins, or the mechanical agent of regeneration.

Paul furthers his discussion of the inadequacy of the Jew's religion by contrasting it with what God really intended it to be, viz., a true religion of the spirit (verses 28, 29), for circumcision is not so much of the physical flesh as it is of the heart. This concept is as old as the book of Deuteronomy, but the Jews had failed to realize the spiritual nature of God's intention for them. A true Jew is one who has had an inward change, which change was symbolized by circumcision. Valid spiritual experience is in terms of a changed heart, not merely changed flesh; it is not outward conformity to the letter of the law, but inward conformity to the spirit of the law. Then will one have "praise, not of men, but of God" (verse 29), which is the real meaning of the word "Jew."

THE INADEQUACY OF EXCUSE-MAKING

The literary form of Romans 3:1-8 is called a diatribe. In all probability there lies behind the written form some real debate that Paul had encountered as he preached in various synagogues. The Jews would violently object to what he has previously set forth concerning the inadequacy of the covenant, of their superior religious knowledge, and of circumcision; and also to his insinuation that they were equally as sinful as the Gentiles. There appear in these verses four definite objections which Paul anticipates that the Jews would raise. He had heard them often before; he includes them here in order to preclude the possibility of rebuttal. These four objections are separate and independent, yet there is a distinct progression of thought that can be noted, for as one objection is stated and answered, the next logically follows and is suggested by the preceding one.

The first excuse Paul anticipates in verses 1, 2. The argument of chapter 2 of Romans seems to lead to the conclusion that the Jew had no advantage over the Gentile. So the first objection is, "What advantage then hath the Jew? or what is the profit of circumcision?" (verse 1). The word "advantage" has an article with it, so it literally reads, "What is *the* advantage. . . ." There must have been a generally understood advantage that the Jew had over the Gentile, hence the definite article. They now want to know about this advantage that everyone understands them to have, in the light of what Paul has recently said.

Paul's answer is in verse 2. "Much in every way, first of all that they were intrusted with the oracles of God." In the words, "first of all," we have an enumeration begun that is not carried on. Paul often does this. He may have intended a second, and a third; but lost in dictation, he does not carry on the sequence. He does list a number of advantages of being a Jew in Romans 9:4ff. Perhaps he had these, or similar ones in mind here, but did not record them. If this is not the case, he could have meant "first" in the sense of being primary or foremost, without any intention of listing others, for this was enough to point up the inherent advantage of being a Jew.

The particular advantage that he mentions is that the Jews had been intrusted with the oracles of God. While God had rarely spoken to the rest of mankind, except in the vague voice of nature or in the obscure accents of reason or conscience, God had clearly spoken His message of revelation and redemption to this small tribe of people here in the corner of Syria. No other nation on earth had been blessed in the unique and distinct way that Israel had. Greece had struggled for centuries to obtain the metaphysical insights that her philosophers had distilled from their own unaided reason, but the Jews had been blessed beyond measure with a clear revelation of spiritual values. This access to a God-given corpus of truth concerning ultimate realities was "the advantage" of being a Jew. However, the Jews failed to realize this great advantage because they regarded the law only as an objective entity to be possessed — it had no subjective influence on their personal lives, save in a very general way. They were the repository for this body of God-given truth, but they failed to let it really enhance their spiritual life. That is the reason why they were not fully aware of the great advantage that was theirs.

There is a similar advantage in our contemporary life that many of us have failed to realize. America has grown up in a revivalistic environment and culture. Especially is this true of the South. In many countries the Gospel is never heard. In many others it is so perverted with sacramentarian concepts that a pure evangelistic and soul-satisfying note is rarely heard. But as secular as America may be, to a great extent we still move in a spiritual atmosphere of pure gospel preaching and evangelistic outlook for which we should be profoundly grateful.

The second objection is found in verses 3, 4. The Jews ask, "What if some were unfaithful? Does their unfaithfulness nullify the faithfulness of God?" The Jews felt that since God had made a covenant with Abraham and his descendants, that they were acceptable to God no matter what they did. They reasoned that since God had made this covenant, if He went back on it because some Jews had become unfaithful, God Himself would also be unfaithful. In reply to this Paul shows that God is just in all His action. He refers to Psalm 51:4 to demonstrate that David was punished, notwithstanding the covenant that God had made with him. The words which Paul quotes in verse 4 suggest a court-room scene in which God contends with man. When He does, God always comes off justified. Israel had misunderstood the covenant. It was not unconditional, but was conditioned on a sincere and moral response on the part of the Jews to keep it invoked. When Israel failed in their part, God was just in changing His action with reference to them without laying Himself open to a charge of unfaithfulness.

As the thought of this section proceeds, there is a mounting note of desperation and frustration on the part of these Jewish excuse-makers. Their tone becomes more vehement and as is usual, their argument becomes more untenable and ridiculous. Note this emerging in the third excuse, recorded in verses 5, 6. Here they retort, "But if our sinfulness serves to show the righteousness of God, then God is unjust to inflict wrath upon us." Their perverted reasoning led them to assume that since the righteousness of God was better seen in contrast to human sinfulness, the more they sinned the more the righteousness of God would stand out; hence the more God would be glorified. However, if this were the case then God could not judge the world, for each incidence of human sin would actually be an occasion of glorification, to which God could not react in judgment; thus the hand of justice would be paralyzed.

The fourth excuse is no less ridiculous. It is stated in verses 7, 8. Similar to the preceding one, the Jews here reasoned, "If by contrast my falsehood causes God's truthfulness to abound, resulting in His glory, why am I still condemned as a sinner? Why not do evil that good might come?" Paul does not even venture a rebuttal for this objection. By this time the perversion of the sin-darkened mind has become so apparent that he just says their "condemnation is just" (verse 8). Here we can see a pertinent characteristic of excuse-making, viz., the longer excuses are indulged in, the more vehement and ridiculous they become. The first of these objections raised by the Jews, in verse 1, is logical and sensible. It shows a clear line of reasoning from the propositions of Romans 2 to the objection itself. Paul gives a studied answer to it. But by the time they have gotten to the fourth one, so absurd and fantastic had it become that Paul does not even reply. He just says that they justly deserve condemnation.

There are other observations about the nature of excuse-making that we can note in these verses. For example, we find that excuse-making is anticipated here as a normal reaction of the sinner. Paul had found in personal witness and in his preaching ministry that as soon as he began to speak of personal sinfulness, the sinner's swift recourse was to make excuses. Even though there is also found here an element of divine amazement in Paul's twice-repeated words in verses 4 and 6, "God forbid," there is a salient suggestion that excuses are to be expected from the sinner hard-pressed by conviction. In fact, excuse-making is the oldest subterfuge of man. It was first perpetrated in Eden when Adam and Eve began to make excuses for their sin. Excuse-making represents the soul floundering about for security. It can no longer rest in self-righteousness, and has not yet come to rest in Christ's righteousness, and so the soul flounders between these two points in the frustrating atmosphere of excuse-making.

Another inference found here about the nature of excuse-making is that each excuse has in it an element of truth, but it is perverted for the sinner's benefit. Each of these excuses has some truth in it, but it is woefully twisted — even to the extent of suggesting that sin and evil are good for they cause the righteousness of God to stand out by contrast. We can see this trait in the Eden record of man's first sin. He was tempted to sin under the guise of acquiring greater knowledge. This was his excuse for sinning. There is an element of truth in this fact; however God intended man to know good and evil from the standpoint of resisted temptation. Man would thus grow in spiritual stature and resisted temptation would result in viewing evil from the height of holiness. He listened to Satan and did come to know good and evil, not from the height of holiness, but from the depth of personal experience and participation.

Again, we can see the folly of excuse-making, for in the answers that Paul gives to these Jewish excuse-makers, he shows that they actually bring God to trial before the bar of human wisdom. Instead of God judging man, man judges God. In replying to God, man reflects on the faithfulness (verse 3), the justice (verse 4), and the righteousness (verse 5) of God.

When R. A. Torrey was at the peak of his evangelistic career, he had a sermon on "The Refuge of Lies." In this sermon on excuse-making, he began by submitting four tests to his audience by which every excuse is to be measured. (1) Does this excuse meet the highest demands of your own conscience? If it does not, it will not meet the demands of God. (2) Does this excuse make you a better person because you hold it than you would be if you accepted Jesus Christ as Saviour? It is certain that an excuse that does not save you from the power of sin in this life, and make you a better person than Jesus Christ could if you yielded to Him, is not valid. (3) Will this excuse stand in the hour of death? A refuge that comforts you only when you are well and strong, but which will not stand the test of death and eternity, is not suitable. (4) Will this excuse stand the test of the judgment itself? Unless it will, it is absolutely worthless, for the ultimate test of validity is not, Does this excuse satisfy you? but, Will it satisfy God?[6] In the light of these very logical tests, the Jew's excuses are shattered, as is every excuse the sinner offers for the delay in accepting Christ as personal Saviour.

There is an inherent danger in excuse-making, for each time an excuse is made a delay in moral action is inferred. This delay is dangerous because of the dynamic nature of the Gospel. You cannot hear the Gospel without being drastically affected by it — either for better or for worse. You will be made better if you yield, but worse if you resist, for by resisting the heart is hardened little by little with each incidence of rejection. This delay is also an affront to God, for to refuse Him His rightful place of dominion is to mock His goodness, presume upon His mercy, and tempt His justice. Delay is personally dangerous because you may come to the end of life unconscious or irrational. Even though you plan to repent before it is too late, a certain amount of rational awareness is necessary to experience salvation, and if in the hour of death you have not full possession of your mental faculties, then repentance is impossible. To delay in the acceptance of Christ is to give sin time to increase and expand, thus to becloud the mind, subvert the emotions, and impair the will. One of the most foolish excuses one can make is to say, "I want to wait until I am better." This is impossible, because any delay will give sin time to grow. You can only be made worse by delay, never better. However, the greatest danger in delay is the uncertainty of death. You do not know when that dread hour may come. Many a person who planned to repent at the eleventh hour died at ten-thirty!

Aware of the sinner's tendency to make excuse and realizing the danger inherent in the delay caused by excuse-making, Paul solemnly deals with the anticipated excuses of the Jews in order to hasten their steps to the point of submission to the fact of their own desperate condition as sinners, and their need of justification through faith in Jesus Christ.

[6] R. A. Torrey, *Real Salvation* (New York: Revell, 1905), pages 97-98. Adapted but not quoted verbatim.

6

A Study in Superlatives

Text: Romans 3:9-23

Paul now sweeps to the conclusion of the argument that he has been pursuing since 1:18, namely, the righteousness of God revealed against the background of human sinfulness. Actually this section ends with 3:21, but since human sinfulness is again referred to in verse 23, and since we wish to contrast the superlative depth of human sin with the superlative height of God's righteousness revealed in justification, we will extend the present exposition into two verses that formally belong to the next major section.

In verses 9-20 we find the climax to Paul's great study in human depravity. He speaks now in terms unrestricted by race or religion, for here he terminates his argument with superlatives, showing once more the universality of man's sinfulness. Then from this dark depth of superlative sin he rapidly surmounts the heights, as he presents in dramatic contrast the superlative righteousness of God in justifying the sinner (verses 21-23).

The Universality of Man's Unrighteousness

Verses 9-20 provide a summary argument taken from the Old Testament and in which he concludes his charge against all mankind. As if he had not said enough in the preceding chapters of Romans to bring every Jew as well as Gentile to his knees in confession and repentance, he once more adduces from Scripture such a pertinent array of texts concerning man's unrighteousness "that every mouth may be stopped and all the world be brought under the judgment of God" (verse 19).

Though this universal depravity is demonstrated primarily from the array of Old Testament texts, in these verses we can also find two other things that contribute to his dictum concerning the sinfulness of all mankind, for we find here an allusion to racial sinfulness (verse 9), and an allusion to legal condemnation (verse 19), as well as the reference to Scriptural witness concerning man's sin (verses 10-18).

The opening sentence of verse 9 is notoriously obscure. This is due to the number of different grammatical possibilities. The question can be rendered three different ways, and there are two alternatives in translating the answer. But whatever rendering is taken, the meaning is essentially the same: racially, both Jews and Greeks are under sin. The word "under" which Paul uses suggests the idea of *dominion* or *subjugation*. This infers not only the guilt, but more properly the ruling power of sin, for sin is not only a series of acts that bring guilt, but behind each act is the sinful tendency which motivates the act. It is this tendency which dominates both Jew and Greek that Paul is thinking of here. In addition to this, the argument is made more devastating by the fact that Paul picks out the elite of the human race: the Greek who was noted for his culture, and the Jew who was noted for his high ethical monotheism. Since no other race had ever superseded the Jew in religion and the Greek in culture, it follows that if their religious and cultural genius could not make them acceptable to God, then all others are swept into condemnation, because no other race had achieved what the Jew and the Greek had. This is the same strategy that Jesus used concerning the universal necessity of the new birth. He did not choose someone who was obviously in need of spiritual regeneration, but He singled out the cultured, religious, moral, scholarly Nicodemus and said to him, "*You* must be born again!" The inference is apparent, for it is the same tactic that Paul uses here — if Nicodemus needed it, then everyone does, for everyone else is admittedly inferior to the religious stature of this man of the Pharisees.

During the lifetime of Christ there were three national forces represented in Palestine. It is very provocative that when Jesus died there was placed on the cross above His head a placard reporting the crime for which He was being executed. The significant thing about it is that it was written in three different languages: Hebrew, Greek, and Latin. Hebrew, the national language, the language of religion. Greek, the international language, the language of culture. Latin, the official language, the language of government. All conspired in His death — an apostate

religion, a corrupt government, and an indifferent culture. However the racial or national genius of man expresses itself — whether
in religion, culture, or government, it is perverse because it is
dominated by the sin principle and thus hostile to God. That is
why Paul says in verse 9, "We have laid to the charge of both
Jew and Greeks, that they are all under sin." The phrase "laid
to the charge of" is a legal term. He means that he has not only
made the charge, but he has proved the indictment, "all under
sin," to be true. Hence, neither Jew nor Greek can qualify for acceptance with God on the basis of their racial qualities or characteristics.

The collection of texts which contain quotations from five
different psalms and the prophecy of Isaiah, may have existed as
a collection at the time and Paul merely commandeered it for
his purpose here, or he may have put it together expressly for
the writing of Romans. The rabbis often did this. They called it
"stringing pearls." These quotations, found in verses 10-18, are
an appeal to final authority. When Paul turns to the Hebrew
Scriptures as the arbitrator in this dispute over self-righteousness
versus God's righteousness, the issue is settled, for Scripture
declares that "there is none righteous, no, not one." Calvin observes that these words in the latter part of verse 10 form Paul's
thesis. This is not a quotation from Psalm 14:3 as the margin
would lead us to believe, because Paul correctly quotes from this
passage in verse 12, and also because the word "righteous" used
in verse 10, does not appear in either the Greek or the Hebrew
versions of Psalm 14:3. The passages that follow, then, have
been chosen by Paul to substantiate his premise: "there is none
righteous, no, not one."

Expositors have systematized these quotations into various
groupings. Most of these attempts are rather arbitrary; however,
they do help us to expound these texts and adequately relate them
to our experience. One of the most satisfying methods of expounding them is to understand that these particular texts have been
chosen to demonstrate that the *entire personality* has been perverted by sin. This would be a double indictment in the charge
of human sinfulness because we would not only see the entire
race under condemnation, but we would also see the entire *per-*

sonality within the individual member of the race equally dominated and condemned by sin.

In the thirteen separate affirmations about human sinfulness found in verses 11-18, we find a reference to the totality of human personality devastated by sin: the depraved emotion, the depraved understanding, the depraved will, the depraved speech, and depraved action. These five specific areas of sin's penetration can properly be summed up in two: inwardly and outwardly sin has radically affected the personality so that internally every thought, emotion, and motive is affected; and externally, every word and deed is under the dread dominion of sin's power. This is total depravity. Not that man is now as evil as it is possible for him to be, but it does mean that every area of life is so affected by sin that man is by nature potentially evil in the absolute sense, and unless he is restrained by God's grace this evil will ultimately end in a condition of determined and irrevocable corruption. Liberal theology has said that there is a spark of divinity within every person that will cause him to evolve into God's complete likeness. Paul says the reverse. There is latent within humanity a force for total corruption which will carry mankind relentlessly into complete degeneration — unless the dynamic of the new birth intervenes to reverse the process.

In verse 18 we find a reference to the depraved heart or *emotion*. Paul, quoting from Psalm 36:1, says, "There is no fear of God before their eyes." The psalmist precedes Paul's quotation with these words, "The transgression of the wicked saith within my heart, There is no fear of God before his eyes." Although in the Old Testament the heart is the center of knowing and willing, as well as feeling, the latter is perhaps in view here because from the heart proceeds the fact that "there is no fear of God" in the sinner. A lack of fear suggests that there is no devotion, no love for God to guide their conduct. Fear is the negative side of love; it has to do with the feeling of awe. Love seeks to please God; fear seeks not to offend Him. When the negative of fear is not present, it is certain that the positive of love is not present either; hence this verse searches the depth of human emotion and concludes that it is perverse.

Although the unregenerate mind of the natural man is thoroughly competent to investigate physical phenomena and formulate an interpretation of it in the various realms of the sciences, it does not follow that the same competency exists in spiritual things. For Paul, referring to sinful humanity, says, "There is none that understandeth." Here in verse 11 the apostle gives the thought and not the precise words of Psalm 53, as he suggests to us the depravity of the *mind*. The image of God which was breathed into man at the creation of his humanity means that at one time man could know God, for the image gave man a rational affinity for God. He could respond to God and have intelligent communication with Him. This is not the case now, for the image of God in man has been sullied by sin. Natural man no longer has the power to correspond with God. That is why Jesus said to Nicodemus, "Except a man be born again, he cannot see the kingdom of God." God's kingdom of spiritual realities is beyond the reach of the natural mind, due to sin's defacement of God's image and the subsequent impairing of the rational capacity for knowing spiritual things.

This same verse suggests the perverse *will* of the sinner, for Paul, again quoting the substance of Psalm 53, says, "There is none that seeketh after God." It is interesting to observe the power of sin in determining the volition of the sinner. It is generally understood that all people have an innate longing for God. This St. Augustine expressed when he said that "man was created for God and will not rest until he rests in Him." However, sin's power is so dominant in human experience that even though a longing for God is instinctive to the soul, the natural man does not actively seek God in fulfillment of this native desire, because his *will* has been so perverted by sin that it naturally gravitates toward evil. Even if the sinner's mind were not beclouded by sin, he could not achieve righteousness through sheer will-power, even if he knew what constituted acceptable righteousness, for his *will* is perverted.

Since all areas of human personality have been affected by sin, it logically follows that the outward life would show the results of this fundamental affliction. And so it does — in both *word* (verses 13, 14), and *deed* (verses 15-17). This Paul demonstrates as he further quotes from the Psalms and from the prophecy of Isaiah. It was Jesus who first indicated in Mark 7:1-23 that it is one's speech that reveals internal corruption. Paul echoes this as he alludes to the various organs of speech in verses 13, 14. "Their throat is an open sepulchre," i.e., their speech is like the noxious odor from a newly opened grave. "With their tongues they have used deceit." The language of the psalm says they have "smooth tongues," i.e., they flatter. This deceitful flattery is an addiction, for they do it constantly, according to the word that Paul uses. "The poison of asps is under their lips." The poison sac of a deadly serpent lies in this area. Thus the mouth of the sinner is filled with the poisonous venom of "cursing and bitterness."

The deeds of the sinner, as well as his words, proceed from the corrupt personality (verses 15-17). Paul quotes freely from the Greek version of Isaiah 58:7, 8, in which the prophet confesses the corrupt ways of Israel. "Their feet are swift to shed blood; destruction and misery are in their ways; and the way of peace have they not known." But these truths are universal, applicable not only to Israel, but to all men; for in verse 12 Paul indicates the universality of these Scriptural quotations: "They have all turned aside, they are together become unprofitable; there is none that doeth good, no, not so much as one."

Verses 19, 20 give us a third argument that Paul invokes in order to declare the universal sinfulness of humanity. He has shown *racial condemnation* and *Scriptural condemnation*, and he now directs his readers' attention to the *legal condemnation* which is also the plight of the sinner. Surveying the Bible, we find that the law of God has a threefold purpose. Its ultimate purpose appears in Galatians 3:24, i.e., to lead the sinner to Christ for salvation. Its primary purpose is to reveal the character of the Lawgiver. However, there is a secondary purpose of the law which is apparent in the epistle of Romans. Paul's words in verse 19 suggest it to us, ". . . whatsoever the law saith, it speaketh to them that are under the law; that every mouth may be stopped and all the world may be brought under the judgment of God." The law reveals sin. The Jew would readily admit the force of the preceding Scripture quotations with reference to the Gentile, but here Paul again brings the Jew into the picture by showing that the law equally condemns him, for before the violated law "every mouth is stopped." This word is fraught with a fierce finality. This is why Paul concludes verse 20 by saying, "Through

the law cometh the knowledge of sin." This is more than intellectual knowledge. There is another word that Paul could have
used if this were in his mind. However, the word he uses here
means *the full realization of an inner conviction*. This is a knowledge that vitally influences character, for the sinner, having faced
the full implication of the law, is stripped of all self-sufficiency.
All men are now silent and defenseless.

In these verses Paul also strikes the death knell to all systems of justification by works — Jewish as well as modern, "for
by the works of the law shall no flesh be justified" (verse 20).
The Romanist and some Arminians have attempted to rationalize
the word "law" in order to continue propagating a doctrine of
justification by works, saying that the "law" in view here is the
ceremonial law. But there is no such distinction in the mind of
Paul, for there was no such distinction made in his day between
the moral law and the ceremonial law. When the Jew spoke of
sin he made no distinction between moral evil and ceremonial im-
purity. That Paul did not restrict his thinking to the ceremonial
law is also apparent from the fact that he does not use the article
which appears in our English translation. He literally says, "By
works of law shall no flesh be justified" — any works of any law.
Thus no ethical or religious principle of works can make the sinner right with God. Since the Jewish ceremonial law has few
hearers today, this omitted article makes Paul's words very relevant
to us in showing that contemporary systems of justification by
works are as inept to save as the Jewish system was two thousand
years ago.

THE UNIVERSALITY OF GOD'S RIGHTEOUSNESS

Fundamental in the theology of Paul is the fact that man
is a great sinner. But he was also persuaded of the fact that Jesus
Christ is a great Saviour. It is this truth that comes to light now
in verse 21. Out of the depths where he has been delineating the
depravity of the human personality, Paul sweeps with the majestic
climax of a hallelujah chorus to the superlative height of the revelation of God's righteousness in saving the sinner. He proclaims in
triumph, "But now apart from the law a righteousness of God
hath been manifest," thus opening the prison door to the doomed
sinner that he may flee the shackles of sin's dominion, and the

broken law's condemnation, into the open arms of a glorious Saviour who can provide for the sinner a perfection not his own.

It is important that we again remind ourselves that the righteousness of God in Romans is not what God *is*, but what God *does*. It is His righteous activity which makes possible the salvation of the unrighteous sinner at the same time maintaining its own essential nature. This is made possible not by what the sinner does, but by what God accomplishes for the sinner, through Christ. It is this righteous activity, made possible by the work of Christ on the cross, that Paul has in mind when he says, "A righteousness of God hath been manifest" (verse 21). With these words he takes us back to Calvary where this righteous activity of God has its historical beginning.

There are three simple facts that emerge in these following verses to help us to see the universality of God's righteousness, or more precisely God's righteous activity: this righteousness is needed by all people (verse 23); it is revealed to all people (verse 21); and it is available to all people (verse 22).

Once again Paul returns to his previous theme as he states in verse 23 the *need* of all people for God's righteous activity to express itself in salvation, because "all have sinned and fall short of the glory of God." The entire scope of human spiritual history is gathered up in the timeless tense of the words, "All have sinned." It looks back to the point when sin entered the human race, it includes the time it entered the individual's own experience, and it infers the present and future prevailing condition of human sinfulness. The words, ". . . and fall short of the glory of God," more precisely look to the resulting present and prevailing condition of the historical incidence of sin. Man was created to reflect the glory of God in his own person. From this potential glory he has defected because of his sin. Man's resulting plight is reflected in the words "fall short," for they suggest not only the fact of sin but also the resulting feeling of destitution, inadequacy, and guilt.

To the sinner who has lost the potential of God's glory comes this *revelation* of God's righteous activity (verse 21). "But now" suggests either a temporal contrast or a logical contrast. If temporal, then it would mean, "But now, at this time." If a logical contrast is in Paul's mind, it would mean, "But now, in the light of man's sinfulness, a new righteousness is possible." It is made possible "apart from the law," for a righteousness revealed under the law would mean only wrath. Though these words suggest that this is a new revelation, Paul hastens to remind us of the fact that it is not an innovation, for it was in the plan of God all the while, "being witnessed by the law and the prophets." These words indicate that the witness of the Old Testament to the truth of justification by faith is still going on. This he will more clearly illustrate from the life of Abraham in chapter 4 of Romans.

Since Paul has excluded the possibility of the law or good works providing this righteousness, it must be posited on some other method of universal accessibility. This universal *method* is "through faith in Jesus Christ unto all them that believe" (verse 22).

Thus, highlighted against the massive darkness of human sin and unrighteousness, comes the glorious message of the righteous activity of God in saving the sinner. Superlative sinfulness has challenged God to superlative activity in affecting human redemption.

7

JUSTIFICATION BY FAITH ALONE

Text: Romans 3:24-30

PAUL STATES THE THEME OF THE EPISTLE OF ROMANS IN 1:17, namely, the righteousness of God. All subsequent material in the epistle is an elaboration of this theme. The first contribution that Paul makes to our understanding of the righteousness of God is to convince us of its universal need. This he does by showing both Jew and Gentile to be sinners. Thus he highlights this righteousness of God against the background of human sinfulness (Romans 1:18-3:21). Having placed all men in their proper spiritual perspective — as to their innate sinfulness, as well as to the inadequacy of their religious works, Paul enters into a new age in Romans 3:21, in which he views the righteousness of God at work providing justification for the unrighteous sinner. This will be his thesis in 3:21-5:21, the second major division of the epistle.

The heralding of this new age of spiritual experience is proclaimed in Paul's words, ". . . being justified freely by his grace" (verse 24). Though justification is one of the most distinctive of New Testament truths, it was not until the Reformation that the doctrine found its classic expression, for up through the Middle Ages this vital truth was woefully confounded with the moral process of sanctification — an error which the Romanist church still propagates by teaching that one is justified only to the extent that he is sanctified. However, the Reformers have clearly defined what Paul meant by the concept, so that we can now approach these verses in Romans with the clear understanding which it took history 1500 years to distill for us.

Justification is a declarative act of God. He does not make the sinner subjectively righteous in justification. He declares him to be objectively righteous, i.e., righteous before the law. Wm. Barclay has observed that when a Greek verb ends in *-oun*, as this word "to justify" does, it does not mean to make a person something, but to treat or reckon him to be something.[7] (It is regeneration and sanctification that actually makes the sinner righteous.) Justification is a declarative act of God that is grounded in the work of Christ. Thus the sinner as such is not declared righteous, he is declared righteous only in Christ. This is the result of grace, not of works on his part; hence the instrumental cause is not baptism but faith. This declarative act of God is instantaneous and complete. It takes place once for all at the beginning of the Christian life and is never to be repeated.

This understanding of justification has been criticized as a "legal fiction" tending to an artificial righteousness. But this impression is due to an abstract method of dealing with the vital doctrines of Pauline theology. His teaching must be considered as an organic whole. When justification is viewed alone it may be confused with an artificial righteousness; however when we realize that God not only *declares* us righteous in justification, He also *makes* us righteous through regeneration and through the progressive transformation into the likeness of Christ (which is sanctification), then this objection is not valid.

Justification is basic because it alone makes salvation possible while at the same time maintaining the infinite holiness of God, for if it were not for justification we would have to lower our conception of sin's complete devastation while at the same time trying to work out our own righteousness. The result would be the Roman Catholic error of progressive justification in which sins committed after baptism are absolved through works of penance, and then after death final justification is brought about by masses, indulgences, the merits of the saints, and one's own suffering in purgatory. It is against this travesty of the grace of God that the Reformers revolted and declared the grand emancipation truth: "Therefore being justified by faith we have peace with God through our Lord Jesus Christ."

THE BASIS OF JUSTIFICATION

This we find in two words that Paul uses in verses 24 and 25. He says we are justified "through the redemption that is in Christ Jesus: whom God set forth to be a propitiation." The divine basis of justification is not found in anything that we have

[7] Wm. Barclay, *The Mind of St. Paul* (New York: Harper, 1958), page 76.

done, but in what God has done for us through Christ. The words that suggest this are "redemption" and "propitiation." There are two words that are rendered "redemption" in our English New Testament. One means "to buy," and signifies the actual spiritual deliverance; the other means "to ransom," and suggests the price that is paid. It is the "ransom" meaning that lies behind the English "redemption" in this verse.

It is the blood of Christ that is the price that was paid for our ransom, or *redemption*. That is why Peter says we were redeemed not with the ordinary ransom of silver and gold, but with the precious blood of Christ (I Peter 1:18ff). The early Church Fathers saw four elements in human bondage: sin, the law, death, and Satan. Martin Luther added a fifth to this list — wrath. All of these underscore the spiritual need for redemption. We are under the dominion of *sin*, which is an organic power resident within each individual. The violated *law* had delivered us to the bondage of condemnation. There is less in the writings of Paul about the *devil* than in some other portions of the New Testament; however, this was one of the first of the ransom theories of the atonement to develop. The devil is supposed to have gained certain rights over the individual which God in justice cannot set aside. God offers Christ in place of the sinner. Satan accepts the offer, but finds that he cannot hold Christ. Thus through this pious deception the sinner is redeemed from the bondage of Satan. Behind the primitive mechanics of this theory there is some relevant truth, however. The sinner is in a real sense under the dominion of the "god of this world" and very much in need of liberation from his demonic control. This is surely a part of the redemption effected in Christ, though not necessarily in the way that the early Fathers conceived it. *Death* is the inevitable consequence of our sin, so it too has us in bondage — a bondage that can be canceled only by the cross as Christ suffers spiritual death in our behalf.

In addition to these four elements of spiritual bondage, there is another which Paul may have had more specifically in mind in this context. Luther suggests that it is *wrath*. Man's sin has incurred the wrath of God (Romans 1:18). It is the revelation of this sin-wrath relationship that Paul expounds in the preceding section of the epistle. He now points up the fact that the process of justification frees us from wrath, for we are now declared righteous and so put into a domain where wrath cannot penetrate.

The second word, *"propitiation,"* is not so easily understood, for its precise meaning is uncertain. The word occurs rarely in the New Testament. Luther and Calvin said that it had reference to the mercy seat over the ark of the covenant on which the high priest sprinkled the blood of the sacrifice on the Day of Atonement. It is so used in Hebrews 9:5. Some modern commentators have suggested that the word "sacrifice" should be supplied here. If this is the case, then Paul would mean in verse 25, "Whom God set forth to be a propitiatory sacrifice." In any case the reference would be to the death of Christ whose blood made an atonement for our sin, covering it so that we stand in God's eyes justified — as though we had never sinned. Jesus suggested the same thing in Luke 18:9ff in His parable of the publican and the sinner. When the sinner prayed, "God be merciful to me a (the) sinner," he used a word translated "merciful," which comes from the same root as the word Paul uses here. He actually prayed, "God, be Thou propitiated to me a sinner." Jesus said of him, "He went down to his house *justified.*" This is more than mere pardon or forgiveness. It is restoration to divine favor.

Paul says that Christ was "set forth" as a propitiation for our sin. These words are full of vivid and dramatic suggestion, for as Paul penned them there was in his mind the great Day of Atonement in which the high priest took the blood of the sacrifice and went beyond the veil of the tabernacle into the Holy of Holies, there to sprinkle the blood upon the mercy seat. There are two salient features about the Old Testament Day of Atonement that are alluded to in these words. First, this offering was *impermanent.* It was repeated annually because it was an imperfect sacrifice and got imperfect results. In contrast to this impermanent work of the high priest on the Day of Atonement is the *permanent* work of Christ upon the cross — for His was a perfect sacrifice and got perfect, thus permanent results. Paul uses a word here that literally means *set forth once for all, never to be repeated.*

The second fact about the Day of Atonement that must have been in the mind of Paul, suggested by the words "set forth," is that on the Day of Atonement the only ministry of the high priest that was not witnessed by the people was when he went alone into the Holy of Holies to sprinkle the blood of the sacrifice on the mercy seat. In contrast to this, Christ has been "set forth publically" as a propitiation for our sin. C. K. Barrett so translates this in his brilliant new commentary on Romans in the Harper series. He states that this translation is suggested by the particular grammatical voice that Paul utilizes in these words.

Therefore our perfect-permanent experience of justification is grounded in the perfect-permanent work of Christ, publically attested to by the open propitiation of Calvary. Because it is of a public and permanent nature, it is freely offered to all, never to be revoked.

The Purpose of Justification

The purpose of justification is to "show his (God's) righteousness." This is the fundamental thesis of all the epistle of Romans, as well as the primary implication of the experience of justification. If this basic purpose of justification, stated in verses 25b, 26, had been kept in mind throughout the history of the Church, the concept of justification by works would never have developed, for justification by works shows not God's righteousness, but man's righteousness. To the extent that man participates in his own salvation through works of his own righteousness, he becomes so much a co-saviour with Christ, in which the emphasis on man's righteousness brings a corresponding de-emphasis on God's righteousness.

The righteous activity of God in justifying the sinner has past as well as present implications. God's righteousness was shown in the past "because of the passing over of the sins done aforetime in the forbearance of God" (verse 25). The word "forbearance" is used only twice in the New Testament, and rarely appears elsewhere in classical literature. When it does, it is used with reference to a "truce," or a "holding back" of hostilities. It does not mean that God did not punish sin before Christ came into the world. This would be a clear contradiction of Romans 1:18-32. It suggests that God held back the adequate remedy for sin until the fulness of time. The *remedy* is in view here, not the punishment due sin. In the Old Testament God provided a conditional remedy for sin; however, He "passed over" sins in the sense of not providing an adequate and permanent solution until the cross solved the dilemma of how "he himself might be just, and the justifier of him that hath faith in Jesus Christ" (verse 26).

But now, "at this present season" the great purpose in justification is manifest, for it provides a solution to the spiritual impasse: how could God save the sinner and yet maintain His own justice? God could not arbitrarily pardon the sinner, for if He did His justice would be violated. If He summarily condemned the sinner, His mercy would suffer. Here was a dilemma for which divine wisdom found a solution in the cross. There Christ dies, "the just for the unjust," satisfying the justice of God; now salvation is freely offered to the sinner, satisfying the mercy of God.

THE CONDITION OF JUSTIFICATION

In verses 27-30, Paul sets forth this condition. "We reckon therefore that a man is justified by faith apart from the works of the law," he says in verse 28. Martin Luther translated these words, "We reckon that a man is justified by faith alone," and since that time "faith alone" has been the unique feature of Protestant evangelical Christianity. The Romanist church attacks Luther's addition of "alone." It is not in the Greek text, and yet it *is* there — the sense is. Faith "alone" must be the sense of this text for all else is of works. Faith is not a work which merits justification. Neither is it a germ from which obedience will later spring, nor is it the equivalent of obedience, for nothing equals the obedience that God demands except the perfection of Christ. Faith in these verses is the unique medium through which justification is granted to the sinner. It has a proper object — the Person of the Lord Jesus Christ. It has a proper content — knowledge and action.

Now these facts are not as academic as they may appear. For they are vital in understanding what Paul means by faith. Its *proper object* is a Person, the Lord Jesus Christ — not merely a system of truth, but in faith we commit ourselves to a Person of Truth. That is why Paul says in II Timothy 1:12, "I know *him whom* I have believed, and I am persuaded that *he* is able to guard that which I have committed unto *him* against that day." Saving faith means an encounter of personalities. Its *proper content* is twofold, both indispensable. First, there is the element of *knowledge*. Faith has an intellectual content. In the New Testament we have been given a set of historical and spiritual data that forms the intellectual content of faith. However, it is possible to accept all of these intellectual truths and yet not be saved, for coupled with this knowledge there must also be *action*. We must act upon the truth that has been given, and commit ourselves to every aspect of it as we understand it. Often we hear people say, "I believe in Christ, but I will not make it public, or be baptized or join the church." This is not saving faith, for it is void of the vital element of action. One can believe in this manner and still be lost. Public confession, church membership, and baptism are not at the option of the sinner. These are not electives in the Christian life. They are part of saving faith, in that they show a willingness to act on all the data that has been given. There is nothing in baptism or church membership *per se* that saves; however, since faith infers an active surrender of our will to God's will, if one says, "I will not do these things," he is demonstrating a lack of surrender, actually an attitude of rebellion, which is the very opposite of the surrender which is inherent in this active component of faith.

Paul refers in these verses to several features of this faith which results in justification. First, faith *excludes boasting* (verse 27). Undoubtedly he has the Jews in mind here. Two articles suggest this (one is translated, the other is not) for Paul says, "Where then is *the* glorying? . . . By what manner of law? of *the* works?" The boasting is well known, as are the works of which they boast. However, these works that result in boasting are "excluded" — shut out by the summarizing force of a decisive act. This decisive act that excludes forever the possibility of works producing justification is the revelation of God's righteous activity in saving the sinner in another way — by faith.

The "law of faith" — more properly "system of faith," for Paul often uses the word "law" in a metaphorical sense, e.g., in 7:21, 23; 8:2 and 10:31 — the law of faith excludes boasting in two ways. It exalts Christ and debases self. It exalts Christ as absolute Saviour. If Christ were merely an example or even an inspired religious teacher, then human endeavor would be necessary to comply with His teaching. Only as an absolute Saviour can man in his weakness and sinfulness respond to Him and find through faith the justification which he cannot produce for himself. It debases self for the same reason. For there is inherent in the very concept of a Saviour the fact that the sinner is unable to save himself. If he is saved, someone else must do it. There are those who claim for the Virgin Mary something that she did not claim for herself — sinlessness. She said, "My spirit hath rejoiced in God my Saviour" (Luke 1:47). In recognizing God as her Saviour, she confesses that she too is a sinner. Only sinners need a Saviour! Thus man is stripped of any semblance of works or merit in achieving salvation. The result is what Paul states in these verses — boasting is excluded.

Verse 28 gives us a second feature. Faith is sufficient for *complete* justification, for it is "by faith apart from the works of the law." This means that justification is *immediate,* not progressive. Salvation by good works, baptism, or church affiliation necessarily infers a delay until these requisites can be fulfilled. But in contrast, justification by faith brings an immediate experience. In a moment faith can make vital contact with God, for it is not qualified by anything of a physical, mechanical, or time-consuming nature. The thief on the cross could not lift hand or foot in an effort to save himself, yet Jesus said he had immediate salvation — "Today shalt thou be with me in paradise."

Faith is also sufficient because it brings *certain* justification. If salvation were by good works, then one would never come to an assurance of salvation because he would never know when he had done enough good works to merit salvation.

Again, the sufficiency of faith is exemplified by the fact that it produces a *permanent* experience of justification. Since justification is not gotten by works, it cannot be lost by the lack of works. Its permanency is resident in the consistency of God's righteous activity and not in our own faithfulness which is utterly inconsistent and which would only result in impermanency.

Lastly, faith's sufficiency is found in the fact that justification by faith is *demonstrable.* Its sufficiency is proved by a resulting changed life. Some have assumed that a conflict exists between Paul and James, the former saying that justification is by faith, the latter saying that it is by works (James 2:20-24). However, Paul is referring to our justification before *God* by faith, while James has in mind our justification before men, by works. These truths supplement each other, for justification by works (before men) issues from the fact that one has been previously justified by faith (before God). One follows the other in determined succession. Hence they are not contradictory, but they logically supplement each other; so if one is justified by faith, this justification will be demonstrated in the subsequent life of good works.

A third feature of faith is its *catholic* nature (verses 29, 30), for God "will justify the circumcision (Jew) by faith, and the uncircumcision (Gentile) through faith." The universal efficacy of faith is concluded from the fact that God is One (verse 29), and thus has but one method of dealing with all people. Here we have the inter-play of a universal God, a universal race of sinners, comprising both Jew and Gentile, and a universal method of salvation — faith.

8

Saved As Abraham Was

Text: Romans 4:1-25

SOME HAVE CONCEIVED OF JUSTIFICATION BY FAITH AS IF IT WERE formulated by the apostle Paul as an entirely new spiritual concept in God's dealing with man, or even as if it were an innovation of Luther and Calvin during the Reformation. However, with the elaborate exposition of Abraham's spiritual experience here in chapter 4 of Romans, Paul carries us back nearly four thousand years as he demonstrates that God's method of making the sinner righteous has never changed. Spiritual experience is *one,* for God has always justified the sinner by faith alone.

Paul's reference to Abraham is crucial to the Jewish concept of righteousness by works, for they looked to Abraham not only as the natural head of the race, but as the spiritual head also. He was the *locus classicus* of righteousness. If Paul can now show that Abraham was justified not by works of his own righteousness, but by faith, then his whole point is well taken.

However, the issue is no less crucial for us, for if Paul can show that Abraham was saved in the same way that we are, then he has demonstrated a vast historical unity in spiritual experience. We do not wish to infer that there is only what some theologians have called "myth" prior to Genesis 12; however the history that does appear in this early section is so inter-mingled with other forms of divinely inspired literature that some say it is not until Genesis 12 and the call of Abraham that we step out on firm and uncontested historical ground. Therefore, if Paul can show that Abraham, the first *undisputed* historical character to emerge in the Bible, is justified by faith, then all, whether they be liberal, neo-orthodox, conservative, fundamentalist, Protestant, Romanist, or Jew, must agree that we have a vast spiritual unity in God's dealing with the sinner, and that He has always justified man in exactly the same way — by faith. The importance of this cannot be over-estimated.

The relevancy of this entire discussion of the faith of Abraham is set forth in verse 1 — "What then shall we say that Abraham our forefather hath found according to the flesh?" Paul uses a word, "hath found," which is the same as our word "eureka." The word itself suggests a completed action, but with continuing results. Paul means that the historical faith of Abraham has continuing implications for us, for it is always an abiding fact to illuminate God's method in justifying the sinner.

In this chapter the apostle makes a negative as well as a positive approach to the spiritual experience of Abraham, in which he shows that Abraham was not justified by works (4:1-8); neither was he justified by circumcision (4:9-12); nor was he justified by law (4:13-17). He then examines the character of the faith of Abraham as he shows its positive implications for the patriarch himself as well as for the Jews, who were the natural-spiritual seed of Abraham, and for ourselves, who are his spiritual seed (4:18-25).

ABRAHAM WAS NOT JUSTIFIED BY WORKS

Faith is an abstract idea and Paul is aware that the human mind cannot long indulge in pure abstraction without becoming confused. So he embodies this concept of faith in the historical example of Abraham, who everyone agrees was the outstanding representative of righteousness. Jesus used the same concrete method of illustration when He was speaking to Nicodemus of the mysterious experience of the new birth. Even the concrete analogy between physical and spiritual birth was not enough, so He made reference to a historical incidence in the wilderness wandering of Israel — the lifting up of the brazen serpent. It was the look of faith that brought new life to the smitten Israelite. Just so, it is the look of faith that brings the new life of regeneration into the experience of the sin-smitten individual. Paul uses the same recourse here by turning to Abraham as a concrete example of righteousness by faith.

In verses 2-8 we find three facts that support Paul's contention that Abraham was not justified by works. The first one is that God is *glorified* in the faith of Abraham. This fact is implicit in the very experience of believing. Now if Abraham were justified as a reward for works, then the patriarch himself would be glorified, not God, "for if Abraham was justified by works, he hath whereof to glory; but not toward God" (verse 2). However, since God was glorified in the experience (this Paul states in verse 20 to be the case), it follows that Abraham is bound to have been justified by faith alone.

Further, it must be concluded from the very *logic of grace* that Abraham was not justified by works, for grace and works are mutually exclusive. While works of merit infer a due reward, grace results in unmerited blessing, for "to him that worketh the reward is not reckoned as of grace, but as of debt" (verse 4). Since Abraham's spiritual experience is one of grace — and Paul arrives at this conclusion from an analysis of the experience itself — he could not have been justified by works.

However, the most potent argument that the apostle uses to substantiate his premise is the categorical *statement of Scripture* that Abraham was justified by faith. "For what saith the Scripture? Abraham believed God, and it was reckoned unto him for righteousness" (verse 3). The faith of Abraham was a familiar topic for discussion among the rabbis. However, they misinterpreted the faith of Abraham in terms of merit. They said that when God saw Abraham's faith it merited the favor of God. But this could not have been the case. Abraham's faith was "reckoned" as righteousness. If it were reckoned as righteousness, it could not have been righteousness itself; hence not a work of merit. The thing that made Abraham righteous was not his faith, but the fact that God declared him to be righteous. His faith was only the historical incidence of the declaration. Just so in a similar fashion we are not saved by faith. We are saved by the object of faith — Christ. Faith is merely the occasion in which the saving power of God becomes operative in our experience.

Paul quotes from a psalm of David (32:1ff) in verses 6-8 in order to further explain the meaning of the word "reckon." According to a principle of rabbinic interpretation, when a word occurred in two different passages, each can be used to explain the other. Therefore the "reckoning of righteousness" in verse 3 is the equivalent of "not reckoning sin" in verse 8. The negative of "not reckoning sin," plus the positive of "reckoning righteousness," equals justification. Abraham was reckoned righteous at the same time he was not reckoned a sinner. It was God who did this. Abraham's "believing God" was merely the historical occasion at which time this reckoning took place; hence it was not a merit, but a medium that permitted God to work in grace, declaring him righteous.

God's method of saving the sinner has not been revised, for spiritual experience is one vast historical unity. He saves the sinner today as He did Abraham four thousand years ago. When the needy sinner looks in faith to Christ, as Abraham looked in faith to the promise of God, at that point God steps in and justifies the sinner, declaring him righteous, just as He did in the case of Abraham.

ABRAHAM WAS NOT JUSTIFIED BY CIRCUMCISION

Circumcision was not a determinate factor in the justification of Abraham. Since it was not, this has implications for the Gentile also, for circumcision should not be made a requisite in righteousness for either Jew or Gentile (verses 9-12). This Paul argues (verses 9, 10) from the fact that Abraham being declared righteous (Genesis 15:6) preceded in Scripture the account of his circumcision (Genesis 17:11). This is sufficient grounds for Paul to conclude that justification is for all, not merely for the circumcised, natural seed of Abraham — the Jews, but also for the uncircumcised Gentile, for Abraham was declared righteous while in uncircumcision just as are they (verses 11, 12).

How gross is the spiritual perceptiveness of man in discerning the deep spiritual significance that is implicit in these symbols, for Paul declares that circumcision, the external sign, is only a seal of the deeper spiritual reality — justification by faith (verse 11). He argues that the mechanical rite has no power to save — it can only speak the language of symbolic confirmation of that which has already taken place. This tendency to pervert the sign into a necessary part of the spiritual experience itself is a danger that is always inherent in religious symbolism. This tendency is exemplified in the Romanist mass which has perverted the simple symbolism of the Lord's Supper into the real presence of Christ, making it an indispensable part of salvation itself. The New Testament intention is that the bread and wine be symbolic — an aid to our remembering the Lord's death. However, the utter simplicity and spirituality of its symbol has been woefully lost in the sacramental mechanics of Romanist salvation. Likewise, the New Testament declares the purpose of baptism to be symbolic (Romans 6:2ff). But again, the simple symbol has been lost as baptism has replaced the Holy Spirit and the Word as the agent of regeneration, or the blood of Christ as the agent in washing away sins.

One of the great difficulties in interpreting Romans is due to Paul's use of the Hebrew Scriptures. We would ask, "What precise meaning did the Old Testament have for its readers?" However, Paul reads the Old Testament with much more liberty. He does not hesitate to put his own interpretation on passages he finds there. This raises real difficulties when the interpretation of some portion of Romans turns upon an Old Testament quotation, as it does, e.g., in Romans 1:17 where Paul quotes from Habakkuk 2:4, and in our current study where he quotes from Genesis 15:6. Often Paul quotes only the thought of an Old Testament passage because he quotes from memory and does not bother to check the reference. This we found in our study of Romans 3:10-18. Here in Romans 4:9-12 the apostle sees deep significance in the fact that one passage precedes another in the book of Genesis, thus grounding an argument for the universality of justification in this fact.

ABRAHAM WAS NOT JUSTIFIED BY THE LAW

Paul's contention in verses 13-17 is that Abraham was not justified by the law. Since the Mosaic law came centuries later, and since Paul does not use a definite article here, he must have meant by law — "any legal system." Of course, it would follow as a relevant implication that if Abraham were not justified by law, neither could the Jew be justified by the law — the law of Moses. Paul's proposition is this: the fulfillment of the promise made to Abraham is a *proof* that Abraham was not justified by law (verse 13). He then sets about to prove this proposition in verses 14-17. He defends his thesis by marshaling two sets of facts.

The first reason that proves that Abraham was not justified by law is that the law would make null and void the promise to Abraham because the law brings wrath, not blessing as the promise did (verses 14, 15). Paul describes the essence of the promise to Abraham in verse 13. God promised that he would be "heir of the world." These words, "heir of the world," probably comprehend all that was contained in the promise to Abraham: that he should have a son, that the son should have numerous descendants, that in One of these descendants the whole world would be blessed, and that through Him Abraham's seed would enjoy world-wide dominion. Now, since the fulfilled promise was filled with blessing, and since the law can only produce wrath, not blessing, it follows that Abraham must have been justified on a basis other than law; hence, Paul concludes that he was justified by faith.

The second set of facts that prove that Abraham was not justified by law is in verses 16, 17. Paul's argument proceeds like this — the promise to Abraham meant blessing to all his seed, natural and spiritual, Jew and Gentile. Only grace, however, could guarantee the promise to *all* Abraham's seed. This is true because Abraham's seed comprises not only Jews, but also Gentiles, who were not conversant with the law at all (verse 16b). Now if the promise is to be guaranteed to all, it must be on a basis other than that of law with which the Gentiles were unfamiliar. Therefore, it was on a basis of grace. We are left to conclude that since grace always implies faith, then the promise was guaranteed by faith. If it was guaranteed by faith, it must also have originated in faith. Thus Abraham was justified by faith, not by law.

THE CHARACTER OF THE FAITH OF ABRAHAM

In verses 18-25 we have a positive description of the faith of Abraham that resulted in God declaring him righteous. A superficial reading of these verses gives us a factual account of the elements which comprise this faith. However, with a more careful analysis of what Paul says, we can trace a deeper meaning. For the apostle actually sets forth not only the *content* of Abraham's faith, but also the *progressive trend* of this faith, for it began in hope (verse 18), and ended in full confirmation (verse 21). Between these two terminals there is recorded a progression in the faith of Abraham similar to that which is inherent in all such spiritual experiences. This interpretation of the progressive development of Abraham's faith from an early immaturity to that of later maturity, is corroborated in fact as we turn to the Genesis account and note the early vacillations of Abraham, e.g., when he took Hagar and with her tried to fulfill the promises of God. Only after spiritual wisdom had progressively matured did he rest fully assured in the promise of God.

There are those who feel that they cannot have a revolutionary spiritual experience because their faith is not strong enough. They fail to realize that the *degree* of one's faith is not nearly so important as is the *fact*. One of the greatest fallacies in the spiritual life is this specter of "great faith" which you may feel is necessary as a prerequisite to any profound spiritual experience. This, in a very real sense, can reduce faith to a work of merit if its intrinsic strength is made the issue. In the last analysis, the thing that makes faith great is not the internal strength of the faith itself, but its external object. Even the feeblest of faith becomes great when its Object is great. The slightest faith makes vital contact with God, enabling Him to work on behalf of the individual. From this point of the weakest conceivable contact, God is given free access to the recesses of the soul. He then strengthens the faith from within, for God does not wait for the individual to produce his own strong faith; God does it for him. This is precisely what happened to Abraham, who "waxed strong through faith," for the course of his faith ran from "in hope believing against hope," to "being fully assured."

We can note the same process in the experience of the man born blind, whom Jesus healed in John 9. Even after the healing, the understanding faith of the blind man was vague. When he was quizzed by the Pharisees he first said, "The *man* that is called Jesus" healed him (verse 11). Later in the same interview he said, "He is a *prophet*" (verse 17). Finally he climaxed his experience by asserting, "*Lord*, I believe" (verse 38). Within the context of this healing experience we see a very marked progression in his apprehension of Christ, and therefore of his faith in Him.

In the context of the spiritual healing of Abraham we can note the same progression. It is this fact that Paul wishes to emphasize also because it enhances the very obvious factual account of Abraham's faith. It is of some consternation to note that Paul says in verse 22 — "Wherefore also it was reckoned to him as righteousness," as if God did not justify Abraham until he had developed a strong faith. However, when we turn to the Genesis account we find that Abraham is declared righteous early in his experience (15:6) — even prior to his vacillation with Hagar. In other words, God works even when the slightest faith is present, as He did with Abraham, and from that point refines and matures faith into a creditable medium.

Overlying the developmental phase of Abraham's faith is the more apparent factual content of it. This we find expounded as the various characteristics of Abraham's faith are set forth within the more subtle context of his spiritual progress (verses 18-22). Paul begins with the faith of Abraham in its intermediate stage. The vacillations with Hagar are past. Abraham now dares to hope. Paul says that he "in hope believed against hope" (verse 18). Two kinds of hope are in view here. In the midst of hopeless circumstances, he dares to hope in God. He can now survey the exact circumstances without having a frustrating reaction that would weaken his faith (verse 19), and he could consider the magnitude of the promise without wavering through unbelief (verse 20), for literally Paul says he "ceased to be at strife with himself." Here is a faith that registers hope in the midst of biological impossibilities. Perhaps it is not the firm and absolute condition that he ascends to in verse 21, where he is "fully assured," but it is a condition of optimism. He can at least consider the facts — he is a hundred years old and Sarah is long past the age of reproductive possibilities — and still come out optimistic in hopeful belief that God is able to do what He promised in spite of these impossible conditions. Thus he "waxed strong through faith, giving glory to God, and being fully assured that what he had promised, he was able also to perform" (verses 20, 21). It is of some import that both Jesus and Paul seem to infer that Abraham's faith and spiritual insight became so strong that he looked beyond the promise to *The Promise* — the coming of the Saviour Himself. Jesus said in John 8:56, "Your father Abraham rejoiced to see my day; and he saw it, and was glad," as if he had anticipated it. Paul alludes to the same thing in Galatians 3:16, suggesting that Abraham realized the reference to the singular, "Seed," meant the Messiah.

Paul now concludes this exhaustive study in Romans 4 on the faith of Abraham by showing that it is germane to our experience of justification, for we shall be reckoned righteous on the same basis as he (verse 23). The object of Abraham's faith was the promise of God. In the immediate context it was a promise to bring life (Isaac) from death (the dead womb of Sarah) (verse 17). Ours is a similar object, for our faith is directed toward God who brought Christ again from the dead (verse 24). But as we have pointed out above, the faith of Abraham may have leaped the centuries to center on the Seed Himself — the Saviour. If this is the case, then the faith of Abraham is not only *similar* to that which we must exercise, it is *precisely* that which is required today — faith in a personal Saviour who was "delivered up for our trespasses and raised for our justification" (verse 25).

9

THE RESULTS OF JUSTIFICATION

Text: Romans 5:1-21

WITH THE WORDS OF THIS CHAPTER, THE APOSTLE DRAWS TO A
close the second major division of the epistle, which he began
in 3:21, namely, the righteousness of God revealed in justification.
It will be his purpose in Romans 5 to describe the results of justification. He will make three master strokes, showing the *personal*
results of justification (verses 1-5); its *chronological* results (verses
6-11); then rising to what many have considered the high point of
the epistle, as he sets forth justification in its widest connotation,
i.e., the *corporate* results (verses 12-21).

THE PERSONAL RESULTS OF JUSTIFICATION

Paul introduces the personal results of justification by
saying, "Being therefore justified by faith we have. . . ," to which
he will append the various personal benefits of the experience
in verses 1-5. The "therefore" of verse 1 takes us back to all that
has preceded about justification, not merely to the immediate context of the last chapter.

These personal products of justification can be summarized
in three words, two of which appear together in the opening
verses of all thirteen epistles which have been traditionally attributed to the apostle Paul. They are "grace" and "peace." Neither
of these words which Paul always uses in the salutations of his
letters can be adequately understood apart from the context in
which they appear here in Romans 5, for they are not merely
the empty conformity to correct letter-writing procedure, but they
are the deeply personal and meaningful results of justification.
The third word is "rejoice."

The first of these great personal results of justification,
"peace," is suggested to us in the midst of a critical problem. The
ASV reads, "We have peace with God . . ." (verse 1). The King

James and the RSV also translate these words essentially the same way. However, the vast majority of manuscripts read, "Let us have peace with God." The difference between these two renderings is the difference between a short *o* and a long *o* in one Greek word. Somewhat oversimplified, the problem is this: the manuscript evidence argues for "Let us have peace," while the context argues for "We have peace." If "Let us have peace" is the right rendering — and it very well could be because not only does the weight of the manuscript support this, but also the particular form of the word itself means, "I enjoy the possession of something already attained" — then this would make justification (and its mental by-product — *peace*) something that Paul is urging us to personally enjoy. It would be a frame of mind that the apostle is exhorting us to maintain. To be sure, this is an indispensable aspect of the personal benefits of justification, for we do find peace and mental tranquillity upon entering into the experience of justification. There are many who seek for peace, but all too often they have been misinformed about how to find it. The modern "cult of reassurance" has directed the inquirer to the by-products of salvation without urging upon him the experience of salvation itself. Personal peace can be found, but it is only found when it is not sought for in itself, but when it comes as the aftermath of justification by faith. Only as a person is declared righteous in the saving and justifying activity of God can he enjoy the psychological by-product of peace.

However, the indicative, "We have peace," rather than the subjunctive, "Let us have (enjoy) peace," makes Paul's exposition more basic, for in this rendering he would be setting forth the objective reality of peace, rather than peace as merely the subjective-psychological by-product of justification. The objective reality of peace suggests the condition that exists between two factions who were formerly at enmity with each other. Sin has estranged man from God. In His death Jesus effected a reconciliation between the two. A holy God and sinful man are now reconciled. The result is a prevailing condition of peace brought about by justification. That is why Paul says, "We have peace with God through our Lord Jesus Christ," for it is the Saviour's death on the cross that makes peace between God and man a potential reality.

442 76

Not only do we have peace through Jesus Christ, but in the second verse Paul carries the benefits of the work of Christ further as he says, "Through whom also we have had our access by faith into this grace wherein we stand." The second great personal result of justification is comprehended in the word *"grace,"* for through grace we have both access and standing, neither of which could we acquire by our own righteousness. This word "access" is made up of two different words. One means *to bring,* the other *facing.* It is used of a person who brings another into the presence of a third party. The idea is "to present" or "to introduce." Sin has alienated man from God. This separation is canceled by the work of Christ, for when by faith we avail ourselves of the benefits of His death, He takes us once again into the presence of God. But not only is the initial access to God inherent in the work of Christ, there is also a secured position in God's presence, for we are also given a *standing.*

There is a substantial difference between our *state* and our *standing* in the spiritual life. A clear understanding of this truth would help many Christians to find an answer to the vexing problem of what happens to a person who sins after salvation. Our spiritual experience has two sides — the *positional* and the *practical,* or to put it another way, our standing and our state. When a person receives Christ as personal Saviour, he is justified or declared righteous, thus given a perfect position, or standing. Now this is a determinate and conclusive act of God. It takes place once at the beginning of the Christian life and is never to be repeated, for our standing is permanent and unaffected by anything that may subsequently transpire in the Christian's experience. What happens then when a believer sins? Does he lose his salvation? No! Why? Because sin committed by a believer after salvation does not affect his *standing;* rather it has to do with his *state,* i.e., his state of fellowship. *Communion* with Christ may be affected by the believer's sin, but not *union* with Christ, for that is permanent. When the Christian confesses his sin then he is restored to unbroken fellowship with Christ again. But during this entire process of the believer's sin-repentance-confession-restoration to fellowship, his standing remains constant. Only the state changes within the context of the standing. The standing remains constant for it is the result of justification — the decisive act of God that declares the sinner righteous, thus placing him in this perfect standing which subsequent sin cannot affect. It is this truth that enhances the glorious experience of justification, for not only is it a gracious act of God that gives us access to Him, it also guarantees a continuing access by giving us a permanent standing.

The last in this list of personal blessings resulting from justification is enumerated in verses 2b-5. This third blessing revolves around the word "*rejoice*." In verses 2b, 3, Paul draws a contrast between the rejoicing that looks to the future and one that has to do with the present. "We rejoice in the hope of the glory of God" (verse 2b). Here again the same problem we noted in verse 1 recurs. Paul's words could mean either, "We rejoice," or "Let us rejoice." The authorities differ — A. T. Robertson says the latter, the ASV and the RSV say the former. The safest thing for the layman to do in all critical matters, especially if he is not academically equipped to make an independent decision, is to follow the standard revisions of the Bible. This we do here, especially since the whole context is indicative. Paul is not exhorting, but he sets forth a factual account of what happens when believers contemplate the future — "We rejoice." Since justification is permanent, never repeated nor revoked, then it logically follows that all believers anticipate the future with rejoicing. There is no lurking dread of the loss of salvation latent here. The believer rejoices in hope because the future is secure.

Paul continues: "And not only so, but we also rejoice in our tribulation" (verse 3). Twice in the doctrinal sections of Romans does Paul turn to the experience of suffering — here and in Romans 8. In the latter his subject is *practical* righteousness — sanctification. In Romans 5 his subject is *positional* righteousness — justification. In either case, if one were influenced by the old Jewish philosophy of suffering which decreed all suffering as the result of sin and happiness as the result of righteousness, then one would have a difficult time reconciling the righteousness he has attained through Christ with the continuing experience of suffering that even the justified are heir to.

In correcting this misconception, Paul demonstrates the positive purpose of suffering (verses 3-5). Here we see a progression toward steadfast hope that is developed out of suffering.

Phillips translates Paul's words: "We can be full of joy here and now even in our trials and troubles. Taken in the right spirit these very things will give us patient endurance; this in turn will develop a mature character, and a character of this sort produces a steady hope, a hope that will never disappoint us." Suffering then is not always the result of sin, but a part of God's positive plan to transform the believer into the image of Christ. Paul further clarifies this in his section on practical righteousness (Romans 8:28ff).

So many Christians fail to understand God's positive purpose in suffering. Often we hear the bewildering cry: "Why did God let this happen to me?" as if God were unfair to permit suffering to come to one of His children. However, as Christians, we will suffer — not as a punishment for sin, but as a positive measure in spiritual education. It is a serious misunderstanding of the providential purposes of God to infer that God's will is for the Christian to always be "healthy, wealthy, and wise." This is not so. God's purpose for you is holiness. Whatever will more rapidly achieve this practical end is employed in the providential workings of God in your life. Since we cannot long prosper in prosperity, God must resort to other means for refining us spiritually. Suffering is a most potent and rapid device to strip us of self-sufficiency, encourage us to neglected prayer, and motivate us to deeper devotion. This is why God so often resorts to suffering as the impetus for our spiritual betterment. Thus Paul's intent is to provide for us an adequate philosophy of suffering so that when it does come — as it will, even into the lives of those made righteous in Christ — we will not be demoralized by it, but will rest in the fact that God loves us and will let nothing affect our lives except by His permissive will. We already have a first-hand knowledge of this love, for it is "shed abroad in our hearts through the Holy Spirit which was given to us" (verse 5). Let this love then interpret all of God's dealing with the righteous — suffering included.

THE CHRONOLOGICAL RESULTS OF JUSTIFICATION

The work of Christ that makes justification an experimental reality is surveyed here in all of its comprehensiveness as

Paul now sets forth the past (verses 6-8 and 10a), the present (verses 10b, 11), and the future (verse 9) results of justification.

Looking toward the *past,* Paul declares that it was "while we were yet *weak*" (verse 6), that we became the objects of Christ's death. This word suggests a moral sickness that renders us incapable of working out a righteousness of our own because we are too weak to break the power of sin, as well as too weak to effect a positive righteousness that would commend us to God. Paul also equated this weakness with a condition of ungodliness. He says "in due season Christ died for the *ungodly.*" This is more than merely being irreligious; it is a positive ungodliness, because not only are we impotent to effect a righteousness of our own, but by nature we are positively aggressive in evil. There is another description of our past condition in verse 10a — "For while we were *enemies* we were reconciled to God through the death of his son." The whole circumstance is summarized in a fourth word that he uses to portray our past condition as he says, "While we were yet *sinners* Christ died for us" (verse 8). Our weakness, ungodliness, and the fact that we were at enmity with God resulted in this prevailing condition of constantly "missing the mark," which is the literal meaning of this word "sinners." It was while we were in this desperate plight, being weak or morally sick, ungodly, enemies, and sinners, that "Christ died on our behalf."

However, these verses suggest more than the fact that we were objects of the death of Christ; they also suggest that the impetus behind His death is the fact that we were objects of God's love. Thus Paul says, "God commendeth his love toward us" (verse 8), while we were in this straited condition. He did not commit Christ to die because we were worthy of His love. This is human logic, as Paul suggests in verse 7 — "For scarcely for a righteous man will one die; for peradventure for a good man some one would even dare to die." (Why did Paul repeat the word "for"? It is possible that he dictated the first line and then felt that he could better express himself and started again. But Tertius, his secretary — 16:22 — had now put the first part of verse 7 on the paper and by oversight it was never removed. However, the meaning is not impaired.) A man might die for another if he were worthy of this supreme sacrifice, but in contrast to this human logic, Christ died while we were totally unworthy! These words are important in our over-all understanding of justification. Some might infer that since God declares us righteous, we then become the objects of His love. Paul's contention is the reverse of this, for we are loved first and then declared righteous in justification.

The *present* result of justification is set forth in terms of the reconciled life of practical Christian living (verses 10b, 11). Paul here deduces from the fact that since God was willing to initiate the process of salvation while we were still in our sin, how much more then will He be willing to further the process and save us *practically* as well as *positionally*. In the past we were reconciled by the death of His Son; in the present we shall "be saved by (margin, *in*) his life" (verse 10).

But what does this mean? In these words, "saved by his life," Paul anticipates what he shall later unfold in Romans 6-8, concerning sanctification — or the life of practical holiness. Here again are the two sides of our spiritual life which we discussed above. The death of Christ gave us a *standing* of reconciliation. The resurrection life of Christ gives us a *state* of reconciliation in which we actually live in conformity to God's righteousness, thus expressing in daily living the reconciled life. Paul suggests the power for the reconciled life of practical Christian living by the words, "saved by his life," i.e., our lives are saved by His resurrection life through the indwelling Holy Spirit. How this is done is later to be expounded by Paul in Romans 8:1-11.

It is important that we keep the issues straight here. It is not justification itself that provides the power for living the reconciled life — strictly speaking, justification provides only the reconciled standing. However, on the basis of justification all else is potentially ours. Thus the reconciled life of practical Christian living will follow. This is why Paul sees the reconciled life as a present result of justification, for it is potentially present in every experience of justification.

Four times the words, "much more," appear in the revised text (five times in King James). Paul is fond of these superlatives, for he is dealing in this chapter with the peerless results of the righteous activity of God in justifying the sinner. As his eyes sweep to the *future*, he sees the fear of death and of judgment gone. His logic is clear and conclusive, built on the simple fact that God loved us while we were still sinners. If, when we were sinners, God loved us — how much more now that we are clothed in the perfection of His dear Son? And if He saved us while we were sinners, how "much more then being now justified by his blood, shall we be saved from the wrath of God through him" (verse 9). With these words, and under the flowing impact of his logic, we are carried along as he shows us the future results of justification — "saved from the wrath of God through him."

THE CORPORATE RESULTS OF JUSTIFICATION

The importance of verses 12-21 has been variously understood. Martin Luther, for example, said they were "an interesting outbreak and excursion." Does this mean they are irrelevant to the thought of Romans? Do they constitute only a digression or a parenthesis? Perhaps they are an epilogue to the preceding section, or a prologue to what follows? All of these views have been urged, thus suggesting the difficulty of this section from the very outset.

However, there are other things that make this section difficult, e.g., the *doctrine* that appears here has been called "original sin," "total depravity," and "imputed sin," among others. Since the doctrine has been variously understood, these verses are also variously understood from a doctrinal standpoint. Paul's *language* is also obscure. This will be confirmed by a glance at the English text. You will note how many italicized words appear here — words that have been added by the translators in order to help clarify the meaning. Besides the obscurity of his language, his *literary style* is markedly difficult. He often does not conclude a thought before rushing on to another, leaving the reader to supply some of the content. Look at verse 12, for example. He begins a sentence that he never ends because he breaks off in the middle of his thought to pursue another thought down a side track. The difficulty in his style is also demonstrated in the fact that his parallelism is not concise. He is presenting a contrast between Adam and Christ, but often he gets beyond strict contrast as he shows the more abounding work of Christ.

These problems notwithstanding, it seems most pointed to the discussion of justification that we understand both the relevancy and the reality of this section, for here Paul surmounts to the great climax toward which he has been striving since 3:21. He now shows that the results of justification are more than personal — they are *corporate*. This means that justification is not only adequate for the individual's need, but it is also adequate for corporate sin, for not only is man the individual a sinner, but the race as a whole is one in sin. Since the consequences of the fall go far beyond the individual to affect the race as a whole, resulting in racial condemnation; just so, the potential of justification goes further than the individual's need, resulting in corporate justification. It may be urged that a discussion of corporate justification is purely academic because salvation must be an individual matter. And this is so. However, if the apostle's purpose is kept in mind we can see the relevance of this discussion, for Paul's purpose is to completely expound the meaning of justification, and in these verses he is viewing it from the height of its ultimate possibilities.

If we are to understand Paul's exposition of the corporate results of justification in verses 12-21, we must keep in mind that Paul is reasoning here within the framework of the Jewish idea of *solidarity*. The Hebrew people never thought of themselves as individuals, but as members of a race or nation. Old Testament theologians have called this concept of racial solidarity "corporate personality." Now, this idea is strange to us, but not to the Jew. Therefore, although Paul's reasoning in verses 12-21 seems strange, it was a natural kind of logic to the Hebrew mind to infer that when Adam sinned, all sinned because the race was *one* in him.

Because of this Jewish idea of solidarity, Paul's view of sin in these verses is that it is more than an individual matter — it is a corporate matter. There is racial sinfulness as well as individual sinfulness. Though this idea of solidarity may seem foreign to our thinking, we can see the substance of racial solidarity in these facts: the race is one in *origin* — God created man. (How He created man is not the domain of theology; it is the domain of anthropology, just as how He created the earth is the domain of geology and astronomy. Both science and theology would have escaped a great deal of conflict if each had kept to its own domain. Science tells us *how*. Theology tells us *why*. When science pronounces on the why of things, or when theology pronounces on the how of things, difficulty is inevitable.)

Not only is the race one in origin, but it is also one in *nature*, for all men are constituted body and soul. The race is one in its *sinfulness*, for all sin is one — rebellion. The race is one in its *destiny* — death. This fact of racial sin and condemnation Paul now portrays in verse 12 — "Therefore as through one man sin entered the world, and death through sin; and so death passed unto all men, for all have sinned." Using the framework of history that he had at his disposal, Paul sets forth the fact that sin has made its advent into the race and has permeated the whole, so that all posterity is affected by this sin which made an early advent into the human racial experience. This means that the human race is predisposed to sinfulness. This sin nature is not a physical entity that is passed from parent to child, but a sinful conditioning that the entire race is heir to and that has become the characteristic of the race. This idea would dispose of an otherwise serious flaw that some have supposed to be in the logic of Paul. Our connection with Christ is purely voluntary, but our connection with the race is not voluntary. We are not responsible for being members of the race, nor for racial sin, and hence we are not responsible for our condemnation. However, if we understand the sin nature as a predisposition to sin only, then our personal responsibility for our own sin is maintained. This sinful conditioning sets the stage for sin, but it does not cause one to sin. It only predisposes one. We sin as an individual choice and therefore are still personally responsible for our sin.

In verse 14 Paul supports this idea of racial sinfulness by referring to another universal reality — death. This proves that sin was in the world prior to the law (verse 13), and that it extends to all, even to those who "had not sinned after the likeness of Adam's transgression" (verse 14), i.e., who did not violate an express command of God as Adam did. Why then did they die if they had not violated a known command of God? Because all sinned in Adam and death permeated the race as a result; hence death is a universal testimony to the fact of racial sinfulness.

Because of the solidarity of the race all were affected by Adam's sin. However, Paul now proclaims the same thing in *reverse* to show that this same idea of solidarity has promise of salvation for all, for just as Adam's sin brought racial condemnation, so the righteousness of Christ can now provide racial justification. This contrast between the racial effects of Adam's sin and the racial effects of Christ's righteousness, Paul sets forth in a series of parallels in verses 15-21. He contrasts condemnation and justification (verse 16), the reign of death and the reign of life (verse 17), the one trespass of Adam and the one act of righteousness of Christ (verse 18), and the effects of disobedience and obedience (verse 19). In almost every incidence of these contrasts between the results of Adam's disobedience and the results of Christ's obedience, Paul goes further in the case of Christ and expands the superior effects of Christ's work.

Having now exhausted the meaning of justification in the glorious array of contrasts and superlatives, and having shown the propensities of the work of Christ for both the race and the individual, Paul draws to a close this section on the righteousness of God revealed in justification.

10

The Meaning of Sanctification

Text: Romans 6:1 - 7:6

The righteousness of God revealed in sanctification is the theme of the third major division of the epistle of Romans, presented in chapters 6-8. In these chapters Paul will discuss both the *meaning* and the *method* of sanctification.

The righteousness that the sinner has in Christ is the result of the combined effects of justification, regeneration, and sanctification. In isolation, any one of these great truths is incomplete and ineffective for total righteousness. However, in combination they present a unity of experience that results in both *declared* righteousness and *experimental* righteousness; for it is justification that gives us a *declared standing* of righteousness, while it is regeneration-sanctification that gives us an *experimental state* of righteousness. Sanctification is the growth and development of the new life that is imparted in regeneration. Paul takes up sanctification in the logical course of his discussion in Romans because it is his purpose to show that in sanctification God now actually makes righteous those whom He first declared righteous in justification.

The *method* of sanctification will be the apostle's concern in the last portion of this section of Romans — 7:7 - 8:39. In the segment that is before us, 6:1 - 7:6, Paul will set forth the *meaning* of sanctification. In the analysis of these verses, a good working definition of practical sanctification soon emerges. It is this: Sanctification is deliverance *from* the dominion of sin (6:1-14) *to* the dominion of God (6:15-7:6). It will be further observed that this positive deliverance to the dominion of God is for personal holiness (6:15-23) and for fruitful service (7:1-6).

Deliverance From the Dominion of Sin

Paul's statement in the middle of chapter 6 gives us the key to understanding the positive purpose of God in effecting

110

practical holiness in the lives of those whom He has already justified. Paul says, "Sin shall not have dominion over you" (verse 14). In the progress of Paul's thinking about the provision of full salvation, he now proceeds out of the realm of the *positional* into the realm of the *practical*. In justification God breaks the power of sin to *condemn* the individual, thus providing a righteous standing. Now, in sanctification, God breaks the power of sin to *control* the individual, thus providing a righteous state.

Although sanctification must be considered as an inseparable part of justification, there is a vital difference between the two in the nature of their duration. Our righteous *standing* is instantly attained when we accept Christ as personal Saviour, because justification is instantaneous, taking place at the beginning of the Christian life, and is never repeated. However, our righteous *state* of practical holiness is progressive in its development because sanctification is progressive and continues throughout the Christian life. It is not an attainment which will remain constant, but a continual state of progressive spiritual growth and development. Sanctification admits of degrees while justification admits of no degrees — it is absolute.

It is for this reason that sanctification is not sinless perfection by eradication of the sin nature through a second work of grace. Sinless perfection via eradication, if possible, would be the equivalent of an attained standing of righteousness, hence making superfluous the experience of justification. This particular interpretation of sanctification (in terms of sinless perfection through the eradication of the sin nature) is not without its advocates. However, it has no warrant in Scripture, nor in personal experience, for it is based on a four-fold fallacy.

One of these fallacies is an *inadequate view of the sin nature*, as if the sin nature were an entity which could be done away with like one would extract a tooth, rather than an innate force which motivates the individual to sin. It is also based on an *inadequate view of sin*, as if sin were a series of acts to be stopped, rather than an inborn drive which must be counteracted by a superior force — the indwelling Holy Spirit. The eradicationist also has an *inadequate view of sanctification*, as if the negative, or ceasing to sin, were the whole. It is this limited view which Paul will dispel in this chapter that is under consideration in Romans, for he shows that sanctification is not only the negative deliverance from the dominion of sin, but also a positive deliverance to the dominion of God, for personal holiness and for fruitful service. However, one of the most serious flaws in this position is the perfectionist's *inadequate view of perfection* itself. God is infinite and His perfection is that of the infinite. We are finite. Therefore we can never achieve absolute perfection, for it is an ever-fleeting goal, both in this life, as well as in eternity. Therefore, because we are finite and will never be infinite, we will never reach perfection in an absolute degree, not even in heaven, much less in this present life.

We are not to conceive of sanctification, then, either as a once-for-all attainment (as is justification) or as a state of sinless perfection. Dr. E. Y. Mullins defines sanctification as "the state of one who is set apart to the service of God, who belongs to God. It also means the inner transformation of one thus set apart, the actual realization of a holy character."[8]

One of the advantages Christianity has over other religions, from an ethical standpoint, is that its ethical ideal is set forth not in theory, but in the concrete form of a real historical Person. We can find out what God intends to do for us by looking at Jesus. He is the Goal to be realized. It is sanctification that brings about this divine and progressive transformation into the image of Christ.

Paul's discussion of deliverance from the dominion of sin in sanctification is centered in an idea that appears 16 times in various forms in verses 1-14. It is the idea of "death." In this concept is to be found the secret of victory, at least from the human standpoint. Paul will later augment the human side — this attitude of death to self, with the divine enablement that comes from the indwelling Holy Spirit. However, for now he is developing the human side, the attitude that the believer must assume if he is to attain to the full potential of this deliverance. Paul introduces this complete deliverance from the power of sin with an anticipated objection: "What shall we say then? Shall we continue in sin that grace may abound? God forbid. We who died to sin, how shall we any longer live therein," (verses 1, 2).

[8] E. Y. Mullins, *The Christian Religion in Its Doctrinal Expression* (Philadelphia: Judson Press, 1917), page 417.

True, grace is seen to abound in contrast with the abounding nature of sin, but grace will even more abound if it is contemplated from the standpoint of complete deliverance from sin, not only in theory but also in practice.

What is the principle that gives promise of complete deliverance? Paul says it is suggested to us in the symbolism of baptism (verses 3-6). It is the principle of *identification*. Because baptism in the New Testament is by immersion, it is a fit picture of the believer's identification with Christ, not only in His death, but also in His resurrection; for if we are "united with him in the likeness of his death, we shall also in the likeness of his resurrection" be united with Him (verse 5). Being identified through faith with the death of Christ, His death under the penalty of sin became ours. Thus we are saved from sin's *penalty*. But this is not all the death of Christ does for us. Our condemnation is two-fold. Not only are we under the penalty of sin, but we are also under the ruling power of sin. This power is resident in our sin nature, or the "old man," as Paul calls it in verse 6. Therefore, when we identify ourselves by faith with the death of Christ, not only are we freed from sin's penalty, but we are also freed from sin's *power;* for His death was also our death to the sin nature. That is why Paul says, "Knowing this, that our old man was crucified with him, that the body of sin might be done away, that so we should no longer be in bondage to sin" (verse 6). The way by which this identification of ourselves with the death of Christ is realized is through the medium of faith. When we accept Christ as our own personal Saviour, we actually enter into union with Him through this experience of faith. Thus His death on the cross becomes our death, and the benefits of His death are also realized in our own personal experience.

Now, this identification of ourselves by faith with the death of Christ is the *principle* involved in deliverance from the dominion of sin (verses 1-7). Having firmly emphasized the importance of our identification with the death of Christ in order that the power of sin, resident in the sin nature, might be broken, Paul now turns to the actual realization of this new life of victory as he sets forth the *practice* of victory in verses 8:14. What is set out in verses 1-7 is already latent in all spiritual experience. But we must remember that what is in potential in the initial experience of salvation must be appropriated to our needs in order to meet the power of sin and defeat it in actual, daily spiritual experience. It is this secret of victory — this practice of actually realizing a death to the power of the old nature — that Paul now expounds in verses 8-14.

Since the believer is not under the law as a method of righteousness, but under grace (verse 14b), it follows that the method of obtaining this state of experimental righteousness will also be that of grace and not one of legalistic self-effort. There are three words in this section that hold the secret to this life of victory over the indwelling power of sin. If these three words are understood and are made the key to practical sanctification, just as "by faith" was made the key to justification, a new era in Christian vitality, as full of spiritual potential as that of the Reformation, would dawn.

The first of these is found in verse 8. It is the word *"believe."* Paul says, "If we died with Christ we believe that we shall also live with him." This is more than a theological proposition to which the intellect gives assent. It is an attitude of faith that appropriates the resurrection life of Christ to one's own personal need and experience. Just as He lived in newness of life after death, so His resurrection life can become ours and enable us to live a new life of triumph. (This truth is also inherent in the symbolism of baptism, says Paul, verses 4, 5.) The particular form of the word "believe" that Paul uses in verse 8 literally means "keep on believing," as a constant attitude. Just as by faith we took salvation from sin's penalty from the hand of a dying Christ, so we now take salvation from sin's power from the hand of a living Christ. The only difference between the two experiences of faith is that deliverance from sin's penalty is a once-for-all act. It comes once in answer to faith when we are first saved. Deliverance from sin's power is continual, because sin's power is continual. Hence, one must constantly appropriate this daily victory over sin's power as he "keeps on believing."

The second word that gives direction to this daily deliverance from the dominion of sin is the word *"reckon,"* found in verse 11. The word itself means *to consider.* Again it is important that we note the particular form of the word which Paul chooses.

Its form is the same as that of the word "believe," in verse 8. It literally means "keep on reckoning."

There are two aspects of this reckoning to which Paul alludes: First, "keep on reckoning yourselves to be *dead* unto sin." This is essentially an attitude in which the believer is constantly to engage. We are to keep on considering ourselves dead to the power of the sin nature. Because in the initial experience of salvation we have already been identified with the death of Christ, this attitude of "reckoning ourselves dead" is what actually carries over into experience that which is present in potential in the death of Christ on the cross and in our acceptance of Him as personal Saviour.

The instructions continue in verse 11, for we are not to stop or to be content merely with a negative deliverance. We are also to keep on reckoning ourselves *"alive* unto God in Christ Jesus." The first is "mortification" — death to self; the second is "vivication" — alive to God (to use the words of A. J. Gordon), both of which we are to reckon by faith to be so in our spiritual experience. Our reckoning ourselves dead actually breaks the power of the sin nature in our experience so that we are no longer under its dominion. The transformation is completed, at least from the human standpoint, when we also reckon ourselves to be "alive unto God in Christ Jesus." This positive reckoning actually brings the power of the resurrection life of Christ, with its resulting holiness, into our experience, and thus we realize a positive transformation as well as a negative deliverance. But it must be remembered that this deliverance and transformation is posited upon our attitude of constantly reckoning it to be so.

However, we are not to understand this reckoning as merely an ideal frame of mind that provides some sort of vague religious incentive for holy living. This attitude of constantly reckoning ourselves crucified with Christ is dynamic, because it is this attitude that enables the Holy Spirit actually to become operative in our experience. This is making real what we reckon, for it is the Holy Spirit who produces this condition of death to self. This Paul tells us in Romans 8:13. The reason why he delays in revealing the divine power of the Holy Spirit behind this experience is because here in Romans 6 he is concerned with the human side of sanctification only, i.e., our attitude of reckoning ourselves dead with Christ. In Romans 8 he will return again to this experience, there to expound the divine side of this same truth.

In verse 13 Paul now gives us the third of these key words which must comprise our attitude if the experimental work of sanctification is to take place unrestrained in our lives. It is the word *"present"* ("yield" in King James). This word appears twice in this verse. "Neither present your members unto sin as instruments of unrighteousness; but present yourselves unto God." The two words are from the same root, and mean the same thing essentially; however Paul makes a dramatic shift of tense in this verse. He says literally, "Neither keep on presenting (same tense as *keep on believing* and *keep on reckoning*) your members unto sin as instruments of unrighteousness; but present (once-for-all) yourselves unto God." The mood is imperative — thus a command to a decisive act of presenting. "Yield yourselves once-for-all and then never go back to repeat the performance" is the ideal he is setting forth. The New Testament knows nothing of the concept of accepting Jesus as Saviour and then at some later time accepting Him as Lord. When we enter into a saving experience it is because we accept Jesus Christ as Saviour *and* Lord, and surrender unconditionally to Him. However, as is so often the case, the believer may take his daily life out of the hands of God and thus, from a practical standpoint, live in a state of partial surrender to the will of God. It is this unyielded state of partial surrender that the believer may lapse into after salvation that Paul is now urging to be rectified by a once-for-all, never-to-be-repeated surrender to the will of God.

In these three words we find the secret of holiness, for sanctification becomes an actuality in our spiritual experience when we follow these instructions and constantly conform to them in daily living. The general attitude is one of death to self, based on our identification with the death of Christ; however, this death is made real and vital in everyday life only as we appropriate the power of His death and resurrection life by "presenting" and "reckoning" and "believing." It is best that this process be initiated in our own experience as we consider these words in reverse. *First,* "don't keep on presenting your members unto sin" (verse 13). *Second,* by a decisive act "present yourselves unto God" (verse 13). *Third,* having done this, "keep on reckoning" that you are dead to sin's power and alive to the resurrection power of the living Christ (verse 11). This is a dynamic and continual attitude of faith and not merely a doctrinal or academic thing. *Fourth,* "keep on believing" this is to be your actual spiritual condition (verse 8). When the believer has assumed this comprehensive attitude with respect to the power of sin in daily life and with respect to what Christ has done to defeat this power, then the Holy Spirit makes this experience actual by the power of His indwelling presence. The result is a *maintained* condition of holiness.

Evan Hopkins, who for many years was one of the leaders in the English Keswick movement (a movement which helped more than anything else to bring this teaching about maintained victory over sin in daily life to the forefront of Christian experience during the nineteenth century) illustrates this truth about the maintained contact with the Spirit's power in his book, *The Law of Liberty in the Spiritual Life.*[9] He first supposes a natural impossibility; namely, that by the one act of passing a lighted candle through a dark room, the room not only becomes instantly lighted, but continues in a state of illumination. If this were possible, the room would not be dependent on the continued presence of the lighted candle for its light, though it would be indebted to the candle in the first instance for the light introduced into it. Suppose that the light represented holiness and the darkness sin. By a once-for-all act the candle dispelled the darkness, just as the perfectionists teach that a once-for-all act of eradication dispels sin and introduces a state of holiness. The latter case is as spiritually illogical as the former is illogical from a natural standpoint.

Now, adapting the same illustration — but without supposing the impossibility — let the darkness again represent sin and the light holiness. When the lighted candle is introduced into the dark room, the darkness is pushed back *only* as long as the candle is present. This is not a permanent condition, but a maintained condition, contingent on the presence of the candle. Just so, holiness and the defeat of sin is dependent upon the constant presence of the indwelling Holy Spirit to make it real. There

[9]Evan Hopkins, *The Law of Liberty in the Spiritual Life* (London: Marshall, Morgan and Scott, 1952), page 25. Adapted, but not quoted verbatim.

is no practical holiness apart from the Holy Spirit and our attitude of appropriating faith. It is a maintained condition, not an absolute one.

DELIVERANCE TO THE DOMINION OF GOD

Paul now takes up the positive implications of this deliverance, namely, a deliverance to the dominion of God for personal holiness (verses 15-23) and for fruitful service (7:1-6). He does this under two figures. One is that of a *slave* or a servant; this we find in the rest of chapter 6. Here he demonstrates that sanctification transfers us from a slavery to sin into a state of slavery to God. Just as sin's slavery was "unto death," so now slavery to God results in "obedience unto righteousness" (verse 16). This personal holiness is the first positive fruit of sanctification. The second figure that he uses is that of a husband and wife relationship which has a *progeny* — "fruit unto God" (7:4). This second positive result of sanctification, namely, fruitful service, is discussed in the first six verses of chapter 7.

In verses 15-23 we move amid an atmosphere of *slavery*. This imagery is appropriate, for it conveys to our minds not only our past condition but also our present circumstances as believers, as well as providing a concrete illustration of this abstract principle of spiritual slavery (verse 19a). This principle of spiritual slavery from which this discussion is formulated is set forth in verse 16, in which Paul says we are servants to that form of dominion to which we present ourselves. Before salvation we were slaves to sin because we yielded ourselves to it. This principle is an echo of what Jesus taught in John 8. He says in verse 34, "Everyone that committeth sin is the bondservant of sin." Here Jesus also forecasts the full freedom from sin that was to come, for He said, "If therefore the Son shall make you free, ye shall be free indeed" (verse 36). In addition to this, He suggests the same method of deliverance that Paul does when He said in verse 32, "Ye shall know the truth, and the truth shall make you free." This the apostle reiterates in Romans 6:17. He says, "Ye became obedient from the heart to that form of teaching whereunto we were delivered."

The apostle in verse 18 gives us the results of this freedom that Jesus spoke of. It is a return to slavery! Paul says, "Being made free from sin ye became bondservants of righteousness."

Note the paradox — we were freed from the tyranny of sin only to be delivered to the dominion of God. This is necessary, however, because man by his very nature cannot tolerate freedom in the absolute sense. He must have a master. Since this condition is inherent in our very nature, then true freedom will be found only in complete mastery by the Holy Spirit.

It is necessary that we keep in mind the progressive nature of sanctification, especially as it is compared with justification, which is not progressive but absolute. This is Paul's further emphasis in verse 19b. The progressive dominion of God in daily living is expounded in contrast with the progressive and ever-deepening control of sin prior to salvation. Before we were saved, we presented our "members as servants to uncleanness and to iniquity unto iniquity." With each incidence of sin the soul is pre-conditioned to yield more easily to the next. And with each act of sin, its tyrannical control is tightened. If the process were not interrupted by salvation, the end would be complete spiritual devastation, for "the wages of sin is death" (verse 23). Now, Paul says that with salvation the whole process is again activated in our lives, only in reverse. "So now present your members as servants to righteousness unto sanctification." With each incidence of yielding to the known will of God we are pre-conditioned to more easily yield to His will the next time; and just as with sin, each incidence of yielding to God serves to tighten His control in our lives. Thus with an ever increasing acceleration, we are progressively transformed into His image of righteousness. This is practical holiness through the process of progressive sanctification. This is also true spiritual freedom — found only in slavery, for it issues not in the abject slavery of sin, but it results in being set apart more and more to God's absolute control and dominion. Hence, Paul concludes in verse 22, "But now being made free from sin and become servants to God, ye have your fruit unto sanctification and the end eternal life."

It is unfortunate that a chapter division occurs here in our Bible, for in 7:1-6 Paul continues his enumeration of the positive results of sanctification. The word "or" with which verse 1 begins usually would refer to what immediately precedes; however that seems to be a forced interpretation here. Rather, it points back to 6:14, because Paul now presents a second illustration to enforce his proposition that "sin shall not have dominion over you." Through the allusion to slavery in 6:15ff, Paul has demonstrated that sanctification delivers us to the dominion of God for personal holiness. He now turns to a second figure — that of a husband and wife, showing that our identification with the death of Christ has broken our "marriage contract" with the old nature and now we are free to unite in living reality with a new Husband — Christ. Therefore we now "bring forth fruit unto God" (verse 4) as the spiritual offspring of this new union. This fruitful service is the second positive result of our deliverance to the dominion of God in sanctification.

The somewhat ambiguous nature of this analogy which Paul uses in these verses is well known. C. H. Dodd has said it is important that we ignore what Paul says and try to find out what he means. However, the difficulty arises from a misapplication of the figures in his illustration. The wife is usually viewed as the believer, while the husband is made to represent the law. Since it is a well-known maxim that death terminates one's obligation to the law (verse 1), the obvious inference of this illustration would be that just as a woman is free from a husband by *his* death, so we are free from the law by *its* death. But that is not what Paul says. However, the problem is solved if we view the husband as representing the old man or the sin nature. The wife represents the believer's innermost self — the ego. The death of the husband is our death to the sin nature (6:6). This death to the sin nature is in view here rather than just the dominion of the law, for without the sin nature the law would have no point of contact in the life of the individual. When freed from the dominion of the sin nature through its crucifixion, we are now at liberty to be united to a second husband, Christ.

This interpretation is perfectly natural in its contextual setting, for Paul intends to show that our liberation from the power of the sin nature sets us free for vital union with the living Christ, so that out of this union a new *progeny*, the fruits of righteousness, might come. All too often Paul's point in the whole illustration is lost in the discussion about what the various figures represent. Paul is not further expounding our death to self and new union with Christ. This he has already done in great detail in chapter 6. His purpose in this whole analogy is to show that out of this new union with Christ comes a progeny. When we were joined to the sin nature in unbreakable bondage, we had children of this union. We brought forth "fruit unto death" (verse 5). Now that this union has been canceled by the death of the old nature, we have been "joined to another, even to him who was raised from the dead, that we might bring forth fruit unto God" (verse 4).

Paul considers his point well taken, for he concludes this section on the *meaning* of sanctification by showing that as a result of this deliverance from the dominion of the sin nature through identification with the death of Christ, and as a result of this new spiritual union with the living Christ, we now "serve in newness of the spirit and not in the oldness of the letter" (verse 6).

11

THE HOLY LAW CANNOT PRODUCE HOLINESS

Text: Romans 7:7-25

SANCTIFICATION DOES NOT COME BY THE LAW BUT BY THE POWER of the indwelling Holy Spirit. This is to be the thesis of the apostle Paul in the remaining portion of our study concerning the righteousness of God revealed in sanctification. Having clearly defined the *meaning* of sanctification as deliverance of the believer from the dominion of sin to the dominion of God (6:1-7:6), Paul now turns to the *method* of sanctification in order to demonstrate how this deliverance becomes an actuality in the believer's experience (7:7-8:39). To be sure, he has already anticipated one aspect of the method of sanctification in chapter 6 as he referred to the concept of death to self. But as we pointed out, this is the human side of the experience of sanctification — an attitude to which the believer must subscribe. It will be Paul's purpose now to show that the real power of holiness is not resident in anything that the Christian does through self-effort, but it is through the indwelling Holy Spirit that the power is found to actually realize a death to self and also to realize the positive works of righteousness.

The human tendency to resort to good works as a method of righteousness was a most prevalent problem in Paul's day, as it still is. Even if a person becomes convinced that salvation is by grace alone, apart from any human effort or good works of righteousness, it is possible for him to lapse into a psychology of good works after salvation and thus equate his progress in sanctification with what he is able to do through his own efforts. It is this tendency which had occurred among the Galatian believers that caused Paul to exclaim, "Are ye so foolish? having begun in the Spirit are ye now perfected by the flesh?" (Galatians 3:3). To which the anticipated answer must be "No!" The same Holy Spirit who effects regeneration at the beginning of the Christian life also effects sanctification during the Christian life. Hence He is the agent of holiness and not one's own works of the flesh.

To dispel this erroneous conception that sanctification comes through human attempts at achieving a practical righteousness after salvation, is Paul's intention in the rest of chapter 7. Through an autobiographical allusion he shows that the law cannot produce holiness in others, for it could not produce holiness in his own life, either before his conversion or after he had met Christ. With this master stroke of personal illustration, which suggests more through inference than through positive statement, Paul now shows that though the law is "holy, and the commandment holy, and righteous, and good" (verse 12), it is yet powerless to produce holiness and righteousness and goodness in the believer. In his positive statements about the law Paul intends to show that the law can only produce a knowledge of sin; but he expects his readers to deduce the obvious from this fact, namely, that since the law can only produce a negative knowledge of sin, it certainly cannot at the same time be a positive method of achieving sanctification and practical holiness.

Paul's discussion in chapter 7 has always presented a problem to his interpreters because of a very basic question which it poses: is this section autobiographical? If it is, at what period in his life is Paul talking about? Even when it has been generally understood that Paul is speaking of himself in these verses, it has not been clear if he is speaking as a Christian or if he is speaking as an unsaved person. The Greek Fathers said that Paul was speaking of his unregenerate state throughout. The Latin Fathers, along with most of the Reformers, believed that he was speaking of the regenerate state. However, if we view this section in the light of the context, and keep in mind Paul's purpose, namely, to show that the law cannot produce holiness, then we will readily see that the sweep of Paul's entire spiritual experience is in view here — both before he was saved, and after he had met Christ.

Paul begins back at the time he was a young Pharisee seeking righteousness by his own efforts. To his utter dismay and despair, he had found that the law could not produce righteousness for him in those days because it constantly pointed out the fact of sin and failure, along with the foreboding implications of spiritual death. Thus the law could not produce holiness in his pre-conversion experience (verses 7-13). But he found the same thing to be true after he had received Christ as his personal Saviour. The law was still a source of frustration in the path of righteousness, for it could not produce a practical holiness in his post-conversion experience either (verses 14-25). He leaves his readers to deduce from this autobiographical reference the point that he has labored to make — holiness cannot come by works of the law; therefore, it must come from another source. What that other source is, Paul will set forth in the next chapter.

So many Christians still labor under the influence of this Galatian fallacy, believing that now that they have been saved by grace it is up to them to "work out their own salvation" through self-effort in order to produce a practical righteousness of their own with reference to their daily life, not realizing that Christian characteristics are never the product of self-effort, but that it is "God who worketh in (them) both to will and to work for his good pleasure" (Philippians 2:12ff) through the power of the indwelling Holy Spirit.

THE HOLY LAW CANNOT PRODUCE HOLINESS: PAUL'S PRE-CONVERSION EXPERIENCE

In order to substantiate his premise that the law cannot produce holiness, Paul now shows that what the law actually does produce is a *knowledge of sin*. It is important that we again remind ourselves that in verses 7-13 Paul is back in his pre-conversion days in his thinking. He is once again Saul of Tarsus, the young student in Jerusalem studying at the feet of Rabban Gamaliel.

There are five facets in the knowledge of sin which the law produces. The first of these is found in verse 7. The law shows the *reality* of sin, for Paul says, "I had not known sin except through the law; for I had not known coveting except the law had said, Thou shalt not covet." As a young Pharisee, the driving passion of Saul's life was to achieve a righteousness of his own, one that would conform to the righteous demands of God revealed in the law. His design on life had met with relative success until one day he got to meditating on the tenth commandment, "Thou shalt not covet." It was then he saw the reality of sin in his own life in spite of all his efforts to the contrary.

Why this particular commandment? If we examine the first nine commandments we will find that they are concerned with the externals of a righteous life. They are commands against idol worship, against profaning the Name of God, against breaking the Sabbath, injunctions to honor parents, not to kill, or commit adultery, or steal, or bear false witness — all externals except one, the tenth. It was when Saul looked within to see how he had kept this commandment that he realized that though he had conformed externally to the law by not committing overt acts of transgression, he had in reality miserably failed; for within there was "every kind of illicit desire," which is the literal meaning of the word "covet" that he uses in this verse. Apparently Saul had seen a much deeper and broader implication of the tenth commandment, suggested by this word which he uses here in Romans. The Decalogue qualifies coveting by "anything that is thy neigbour's" (Exodus 20:17). Here in Romans 7 Paul leaves off these objects because he had seen the true spiritual intent of the command, and with this revelation of all his illicit desire, he had also seen himself a sinner and the carefully constructed framework of his own righteousness came crashing down around him. The law had therefore shown him the deep reality of innate sin, not the way of righteousness.

It is not without significance that Jesus apparently used the same approach to reveal to the rich young ruler the fact of his own sinfulness and need. When the young ruler came to Jesus, he said, "Good Master, what shall I do to inherit eternal life?" Jesus answered, "Why callest thou me good? There is none good, save one, even God." Then Jesus said to him, "Keep the law." The young man replied, "This I have done from my youth up." He did not realize his sinfulness yet, for he was probably doing just what Saul of Tarsus was doing about that same time — looking at his external conformity to the first nine commandments. Then Jesus said to him, "Go, sell what you have and give it to the poor." With this brilliant stroke, Jesus brought him face to face with the lurking sin of covetousness, for he saw that he loved his possessions more than he loved anything else. Thus deep within he was filled with "every kind of illicit desire," as Paul also said that he was.

We can see the dramatic and extensive results of this sin

of covetousness in the experience of the rich young ruler, for actually he was guilty of violating the entire Decalogue. The Ten Commandments can be divided into two groups: man's relation to God, commandments 1-4; and man's relation to other people, commandments 5-10. The rich young ruler loved his possessions more than he loved God, thus violating the first four. He loved his possessions more than he loved other people, thus violating the last six. The spiritual logic of Jesus caused this young ruler — a religious leader in his community, for he was a synagogue official — to realize that he had not kept the law from his youth up; rather, he had completely failed to do so. The result was exactly what Paul also found, namely, "the commandment which was unto life, this I found to be unto death" (Romans 7:10). The rich young ruler went away sorrowful. However, Saul of Tarsus accepted Jesus Christ as Saviour and found in Him a freely provided righteousness — one which he had tried all of his life to earn.

Paul's unstated point becomes apparent — if the law shows the reality of sin in one's life, it cannot at the same time be a positive motive and incentive in producing holiness.

Next, Paul suggests that the law gives knowledge of the *nature* of sin, through its unexpected capacity to incite sin into action. The law *defines* sin, but it also *provokes* sin. In turn, sin activates itself in insurrection against the law — thus showing the essential nature of sin to be rebellion. It is a characteristic of human nature to desire that which is forbidden. Taking advantage of this fact of psychology, sin expresses itself through this desire to have that which is forbidden, and hence causes man to rebel against the will of God as it is expressed in the law.

Paul indicated the rebellious nature of sin in verse 8 when he says that sin "finding occasion wrought in me through the commandment (against coveting) all manner of coveting, for apart from the law sin is dead." The words, "finding occasion," were used in a military sense, meaning "a base of operation." In a moral sense, sin exists in the human experience but it did not have a base of operation in the life until the law produced the means whereby rebellion might take place. That is why Paul says, "Apart from the law sin is dead," i.e., sin has no power to express itself (itself being rebellion) except there be a law to rebel against. Here then is a universal dilemma. The law tells us what sin is, but at the same time it is defining sin, it also incites sin into action, for it gives sin an occasion to express its rebellious nature. It is because of this potential of the law to provoke sin that it cannot at the same time be a means of holiness for the believer.

In verse 9 Paul shows that the law also produces a knowledge of the *consequences* of sin — death. Therefore, it can never give the reverse, an assurance of spiritual life. As Paul reflects on his past experience, he observes that "I was alive apart from the law once. . . ." Prior to that day when the full spiritual import of the law was revealed to him, he was alive in the sense that he felt that he was making progress in the spiritual life through his own works of righteousness. But then the day came when he saw the spiritual significance of the law, made plain by the tenth commandment against covetousness; the result — "sin revived, and I died." Actually it was the shocking realization that he was a sinner that he speaks of under the figure of "death." When sin revived in his consciousness and he became rationally aware of its presence through the law, he died, i.e., he also realized his spiritual condition to be one of death. Apparently, he realized for the first time that all his good works of righteousness could not make him acceptable to God because of this fundamental flaw in his spiritual condition — he was dead! His condition at this time was analogous to one who ties apples on a dead tree. The semblance of life is there in the fruit, but the tree remains dead all the while. Just so, his good works may bear the semblance of spiritual life and vitality, but all the while he was spiritually dead. It was the law that finally brought him to this devastating realization of the consequences of his sin. Being spiritually dead, what he needed was something more basic than good works; he needed new life. It was not until he met the Saviour on the Damascus road that he experienced this new life.

Physical and spiritual death are inseparable in the consequences of sin. Both mean separation. Physical death is the separation of the soul from the body. Spiritual death is the separation of the soul from God. Sin is the thing that disturbs either of these vital unions. The image of God in man may mean that man is what he is, not because of any inherent dignity of his own, but because of his relation to God. When man sins, this dignity given to him by virtue of his relation to God is shattered. Thus spiritual death (separation) is the result which inevitably follows. This spiritual death then is the loss of an essential dignity which became man's when the image of God was breathed into him. It is also this essential dignity that is restored by the new birth.

But in what sense is physical death also the consequences of sin? If man had never sinned, would he have been undying? The answer is not a simple "yes" or "no." The story in Genesis sets forth physical death as the consequences of sin as well as spiritual separation from God. However, death is also a law of organic nature. Because man is a part of the organic world of nature, he is subject to physical death no matter what his spiritual condition might be. But we must go further. Man is not only a physical being, thus subject to the laws of the organic world, and so subject to physical death; but man is also a spiritual being, and hence subject to a higher relation than that which is restricted to a merely natural being. As a spiritual being, man was intrusted with the potentiality of being undying. If man had used his divinely endowed spiritual powers aright, he might not have suffered physical death, but may have completely transcended it. He was not created immortal but "immortable," i.e., capable of not dying. A. B. Davidson puts it very strikingly, "He was made capable of not dying, that he should become not capable of dying."[10] But the issue is purely academic, for man did sin and he does die physically. All mankind is now under the dual power of death, both physically and spiritually. It is this fact that Paul became aware of through the law.

If the law then shows us the consequences of sin to be death, it is impossible for it to be the medium of sanctification at the same time.

Sin's power to corrupt does not extend only to its devastation of the human personality by separating man from God and thus relieving him of the only thing that gives him dignity, but sin also has power to corrupt the very law itself. This is Paul's next observation about the nature of the law in verse 10, i.e., it gives a knowledge of the *corruption* of sin. As the law was originally conceived, it was theoretically possible for one to be saved by keeping it. This is the simple testimony of the Eden story,

[10] A. B. Davidson, *The Theology of the Old Testament* (Edinburgh: T & T Clark, 1904), page 439.

for in it there is the elementary expression of law in the prohibition against partaking of the fruit. However, this is not the case now, for sin has corrupted this initial capacity of the law to save and has perverted the law from a medium of life into a medium of death. Paul says, "The commandment, which was unto life, this I found to be unto death" (verse 10). As a Pharisee Paul had labored to keep the law because he believed this to be the way to spiritual life. But when he realized the law was not "unto life" but "unto death," he saw the complete devastating power of sin, for it had not only corrupted him personally, it had also corrupted the law itself by making it a thing of death to all who chose this legal way as a way of righteousness.

Once more we are to draw the practical inference — since sin has corrupted the law, making it an instrument of death, the law is certainly not to be the practical means of holiness for the believer.

In verse 11 there appears a word that is the same as the one used in the Greek version of Genesis 3:13. It is the word "beguiled." Paul says, "For sin, finding occasion, through the commandment beguiled (deceived) me, and through it slew me." Against the background of the Fall recorded in Genesis, Paul sets forth another facet of sin which the law reveals. It is sin's *deceitfulness*. The potential of sin, in the person of the serpent, was in the Garden of Eden all the while, but it did not find an occasion to deceive Adam and Eve until the law of God forbade them to eat of the fruit. "Finding occasion through the commandment," it deceived them, just as Paul says that it deceived him; for though the potential of sin was in his life all the time, it did not activate itself until Paul became conscious of the law. Taking this occasion, "it slew me," he says. Since sin is rebellion, it must have something to rebel against. Though there is a spiritual death that the race as a whole is heir to — this we found in Romans 5:12ff — this death does not become apparent in the individual's life until he personally participates in rebellion. This he cannot do until he becomes aware of the law, for he must have an object for his rebellion. But once aware of the law, which at first seems to have promise of life, he soon rebels against it. It is at this point of rebellion against the law that spiritual death sets in. It is in this sense that Paul means that he was slain. However, the *law* did not slay him; sin did. The law was merely the occasion at which this slaying took place. From this we are to conclude that if the law is an occasion of death, it certainly cannot be an occasion for promoting holiness in the life of the believer.

Paul concludes the analysis of his pre-conversion experience with the law by reminding his readers that though the law is responsible for revealing these various elements of sin in his own life — e.g., the reality of sin, the rebellion of sin, the consequences of sin, the corruption of sin, and the deceitfulness of sin — the law is still "holy, and righteous, and good" (verse 12). How can he maintain this position in the light of all that the law has occasioned in his experience? He tells us how in verse 13. The law is good in spite of all that he has said about it because without the law we could not so clearly detect the presence of sin. It was present all the time, working death, as he has already demonstrated in Romans 5:13, "For until the law sin was in the world," i.e., before the law sin was in the world, producing death as a witness to its presence. But it did not become obvious until the law marked it out clearly for what it is, for it was "through the commandment" that sin became "exceedingly sinful" (verse 13).

Paul leaves us to draw the inference he wishes us to make from this whole discussion of the place of the law in his pre-conversion experience. Since the law, even though it is holy, could not provide holiness for Paul before he met Christ, even though he tried desperately through his own efforts to abide by it, it will not produce holiness in our lives, try as we may "to live up to it." Sanctification must be derived from an impetus other than that of trying to keep the law ourselves.

THE HOLY LAW CANNOT PRODUCE HOLINESS: PAUL'S POST-CONVERSION EXPERIENCE

In order to make the case in point even more clear, Paul turns to another area of his spiritual autobiography to show that even after he had become a Christian the holy law was equally impotent to produce holiness in this phase of his life. This we find in verses 14-25. In these verses Paul describes himself as a Christian trying to achieve holiness through self-effort, but he is beaten back at every turn by the power of indwelling sin. It is this power of indwelling sin that subverts any attempt to conform to the holy law and thus find real holiness through self-effort. It is important to note the studied contrast between the power of indwelling sin in chapter 7 and the power of the indwelling Holy Spirit in chapter 8. (In chapter 7 the Holy Spirit is unmentioned, while the pronoun "I" appears around 25 times. In chapter 8 the previously unmentioned Holy Spirit is referred to around 20 times.) In this contrast Paul now leads the believer to the secret of victory. For, though the power of indwelling sin hinders the self-achievement of holiness, the indwelling Holy Spirit makes it a dynamic reality by producing in us what we cannot achieve for ourselves.

Because Paul's point in this section is clear, namely, that the power of indwelling sin prevents even the Christian from achieving holiness by self-effort; and yet his terminology is unclear, especially in the older versions of the Bible, perhaps the best way to understand this section is to outline the reasons that he gives for this situation. This has been the standard treatment of this section by many of Paul's interpreters, e.g., Godet, Lange, Griffith-Thomas. Paul is systematic in his treatment of three reasons why the law cannot sanctify the believer. He states the reason, gives a proof, and then draws a conclusion.

Here they are in the RSV:

I. *First reason* why the law cannot sanctify the believer.

Reason Stated: "We know that the law is spiritual, but I am carnal, sold under sin" (verse 14).

Proof Given: "I do not understand my own actions. For I do not do what I want, but I do the very thing I hate. Now if I do what I do not want, I agree that the law is good" (verses 15, 16).

Conclusion: "So it is no longer I that do it, but sin which dwelleth within me" (verse 17).

II. *Second reason* why the law cannot sanctify the believer.

Reason Stated: "For I know that nothing good dwells within me, that is, in my flesh" (verse 18a).

Proof Given: "I can will what is right, but I cannot do it. For I do not do the good I want, but the evil I do not want is what I do" (verses 18b, 19).

Conclusion: "Now if I do what I do not want, it is no longer I that do it, but sin which dwells within me" (verse 20).

III. *Third reason* why the law cannot sanctify the believer.

Reason Stated: "So I find it to be a law (principle) that when I want to do right, evil lies close at hand" (verse 21).

Proof Given: "For I delight in the law of God, in my inmost self, but I see in my members another law (principle) at war with the law (principle) of my mind and making me captive to the law of sin which dwells in my members" (verses 22, 23).

Conclusion: "Wretched man that I am! Who shall deliver me from this body of death? Thanks be to God through Jesus Christ our Lord!" (verses 24, 25a).[11]

The law is spiritual but because the believer still has the sin nature to contend with, even after the new birth, there is therefore an important lack of affinity for, and basic antagonism to, that which is spiritual, e.g., the law. Paul states this when he says, "I am carnal, sold under sin" (i.e., the indwelling dominion of sin for this is a metaphor of slavery), verse 16. This carnal versus the spiritual, which is the believer's status, results in all sorts of irrational acts — "I do not understand my own actions"; hated acts — "I do the very thing that I hate"; and paradoxical acts — consenting "that the law is good" even while doing the very opposite (verses 15, 16). Paul's conclusion is that he has not yet found complete spiritual liberty, even though the new birth has taken place — for the new birth can implant the *desire* for righteous living, but it cannot of itself impart the *power* to achieve that which is desired, due to the still remaining influence of indwelling sin.

Besides the spiritual nature of the law and the carnal tendencies of even the regenerate child of God, the law cannot produce holiness because "nothing good dwells within me, that is, in my flesh" (verse 18). Paul does not define what he means by "flesh," nor is he always consistent in the use of this term. He does not mean what the Greeks meant by it, namely, that the material is inherently evil. This would make God the creator of evil because He is the creator of the world of material reality. By "flesh" Paul means man's lower nature (which is in opposition to the divine) where sin manifests itself. The will is the seat of

[11] *Revised Standard Version of the Holy Bible* (New York: Thomas Nelson & Sons; copyright 1946 and 1952 by the Division of Christian Education of the National Council of Churches).

sin, the flesh is the occasion of sin. When Paul looks at the flesh he finds that it is the place where sin manifests itself, and hence not the place where the works of the law are, nor can be manifest. He may desire what is right as a result of regeneration (verses 18b, 19), but he cannot achieve it because of the flesh which always is inclined towards sin, not righteousness (verse 20).

When the new birth takes place, the sin nature is not removed or changed. It will dwell with the believer throughout life — "evil lies close at hand," Paul says (verse 21). It is this "law" or principle of the ever-present sin nature that makes holiness an impossible achievement for the believer who tries to keep the law in self-effort. Because of the presence of these two natures in the child of God, there is a constant struggle, a "war" (verse 22), between the two. However, the sin nature always wins, "making me captive to the law of sin," Paul says in verse 23.

The apostle concludes that the situation is hopeless. He cannot achieve righteousness as a result of merely desiring to keep the law, even though this desire is produced by the new birth. Thus he cries, "Wretched man that I am! Who will deliver me from this body of death?" (verse 24).

At this point he arises to anticipate the great victory over indwelling sin that is not to come by the law, but which is to come by the indwelling Holy Spirit. He cries, "Thanks be to God through Jesus Christ our Lord!" (verse 25a). Sanctification can be a real experience! Deliverance from the power of sin can be known! Positive holiness in daily life can be achieved! However, it will not come through our own feeble attempts to keep the law. It must come from God, through Jesus Christ, by the Holy Spirit.

12

The Sinner's Sanctuary

Text: Romans 8:1-39

"There is therefore now no condemnation to them that are in Christ Jesus." These opening words of chapter 8 give promise of solution to the problem raised in the preceding chapter, where the apostle surveys a dilemma in which each child of God finds himself. The problem is this — with the new birth there comes new life from Christ. Divine nature (II Peter 1:4) is imparted to the believing sinner (John 1:12). This experience of regeneration imparts a new directive to the sinner, for a corollary of the new birth is a brand new set of holy desires. Where once one desired only to indulge in sin, being so motivated by the unrestrained sin nature, the believer now desires righteousness, because he is motivated by the new spiritual dynamic which is the result of regeneration (II Corinthians 5:17).

But the problem that Paul encountered at this point and which lies behind the conflict depicted in 7:14ff, is similar to that which every believer soon encounters after being born again. The new birth can impart only the *desire* for righteousness. It cannot give the *power* to achieve this righteousness in daily living. The reason why it cannot give the actual power for holiness of life is because of the still remaining influence of the sin nature. Hence there is a constant struggle and conflict within the child of God — wanting to do what is right because of the new nature, yet powerless to do it because he is constantly being defeated by the power of the old nature (cf. Galatians 5:17). This is the reason why the believer cannot find holiness through the law, i.e., through his own attempts at conformity to the law. Not only is the law powerless to produce holiness for the reason that Paul demonstrated in 7:7ff (because the law can only point out sin and not the reverse, the way of holiness), but the law is equally impotent to produce holiness in the Christian because of his powerlessness to abide by it, even though he desires to do so because of the influence of the new birth.

If complete victory is to be experienced, then the believer must not only have a *desire* for holiness, but he must also have *power* to achieve that which is desired. In Romans 8 Paul now complements desire with power. For, where the desire for righteousness is given through the new birth, power for righteousness is given through the indwelling Holy Spirit.

The "no condemnation" with which Paul introduces this chapter is not a reference to eternal condemnation. That is already settled in justification. Paul has adequately described this phase of condemnation in 3:21 - 5:21. God declares us righteous and will never again confront us with our sin which might result in eternal condemnation. The condemnation that Paul now has in mind is a condemnation of daily life by the power of sin, not a condemnation of soul by the penalty of sin. Where justification gave us a *standing* in righteousness, Paul is now going to show that sanctification, through the power of the indwelling Holy Spirit, will give us a *state* of righteousness. In this practical state of righteousness, we now live daily under the dominion, not of sin's power, but of the powerful Holy Spirit, hence to know as an experimental reality "no condemnation" in Christ Jesus, through sanctification of the Holy Spirit. Therefore, there is "no condemnation" in Christ *positionally*. This is justification (as opposed to being in Adam). There is "no condemnation" in Christ *practically*. This is sanctification (as opposed to being in self). ·

Romans 8 will present four new areas of spiritual conquest which are made a reality by the indwelling Holy Spirit. They are: a new life of victory (verses 1-11); a new realization of sonship (verses 12-17a); a new philosophy of suffering (verses 17b-30); and a new song of triumph (verses 31-39).

A NEW LIFE OF VICTORY

In verses 1-11 Paul sets forth the dramatic new truth that the previous two chapters of Romans have been anticipating — complete victory over the power of indwelling sin by the indwelling Holy Spirit. This new life of victory contains three elements of truth which comprise the secret of holiness — a new *liberation* (verses 1-4); a new *motivation* (verses 5-9a); and a new *inhabitation* (verses 9b-11). It is imperative that the believer understand these three propositions if he is to live a life of complete victory over sin and if he is to know positive daily advancement in practical holiness. It is for this reason that verses 1-11 are the most important in the New Testament for the Christian. Fail to understand and hence appropriate what is taught here, and the believer's life will remain in the stagnant conflict that Paul described in the previous chapter. There will be little evidence of spiritual development, even though one may be a Christian for many years.

In verses 1-4 the apostle describes the two-fold nature of this new *liberation*. It is first of all a liberation which sets the believer "free from the law of sin and death," i.e., free from the dominating principle of sin, resident in the sin nature, which issues in death (verse 2). It is the "law of the spirit of life in Christ Jesus" that accomplishes this for the believer. Here is one of the most important and meaningful statements that ever flowed from the pen of the apostle Paul — the Holy Spirit's power liberates the Christian from the dominion of sin, thus making the fruits of spiritual life to be the daily fare of the child of God, rather than the fruits of spiritual death. Many shrink from the clear implications of this truth. Nevertheless, Paul categorically declares that it is feasible for a Christian to live day by day with constant victory over sin, made possible through the abiding presence of the Holy Spirit, whose power is sufficient to effect for the believer a victory which he cannot achieve for himself.

When we couple the *divine power for victory*, revealed in this verse, with what we have already noted to be the *human condition of victory* in 6:1-14, we now have the whole picture of the way of real holiness in the Christian life. From the human standpoint we are to reckon ourselves dead (6:11); from the divine standpoint the Holy Spirit then delivers us, consequent upon our believing, yielding attitude of reckoning ourselves dead to self — for it is the Holy Spirit who makes real what we reckon.

Behind this work of the Spirit in breaking the power of indwelling sin is the work of Christ which makes it all possible in the first place. Paul reminds us of this in verse 3 — "For what the law could not do in that it was weak through the flesh." This was Paul's whole argument in chapter 7 — "God sending his own son, in the likeness of sinful flesh, and for sin, condemned sin in the flesh." Paul uses the same word here that was often used in the Greek version of the Old Testament to translate a Hebrew word which means "sin offering." Christ by His death on the cross became a sin offering, thus condemning it. Since sin is condemned, it can no longer condemn us, neither in an eternal sense, nor in a present sense. That is why Paul begins this section, "There is therefore now no condemnation to them that are in Christ Jesus." With verse 3 Paul carries our thinking about the life of no condemnation back beyond the more immediate and subjective work of the Holy Spirit to the historical and objective work of Christ on the cross. He does this in order to ground our thinking in the fact that this personal deliverance, which is produced by the Holy Spirit in us, is actually the Spirit's work of carrying over into human experience that which was first achieved by Christ in His death; for it is the office work of the Holy Spirit to make actual in personal experience that which Christ has first made actual in historical experience.

However, the Holy Spirit does not merely rest with breaking the power of indwelling sin in the believer; He proceeds to produce the positive fruits of righteousness, "that the ordinance of the law might be fulfilled in us," Paul says in verse 4. Indwelt by the Holy Spirit, the Christian is now able to keep the requirements of the law. This is one reason why Jesus said that He came not to destroy the law but to fulfill it (Matthew 5:17). He fulfilled it in His own life and now makes it possible for it to be fulfilled in the lives of His followers through the power of His indwelling presence by the Holy Spirit.

Why then do not all Christians live this life of victory over sin in conformity to the law? It is not because the potentiality for such spiritual consistency is not present in each Christian, for it is. This experience of complete victory is inherent in every experience of salvation, for every believer receives the Holy Spirit when he is born again. Each believer can know this rich life of holiness, but many fail to do so because of the point that Paul makes in verse 4. This life of victory can be known only when one walks "not after the flesh but after the Spirit." This walk in the Spirit means at least two things: *first*, an attitude of death to self. This we noted in 6:1-14. Paul again refers to it in Galatians 5:24. He says, "And they that are of Christ Jesus have crucified the flesh with the passions and lusts thereof" (cf. Galatians 2:20).

Second, it means a positive and complete surrender to the absolute control of the Holy Spirit. "Walk in the Spirit," i.e., fully surrendered to the Spirit, "and ye shall not fulfill the lust of the flesh," Paul says in Galatians 5:16. This dual attitude is necessary in order that the believer might know full victory over sin, plus progressive holiness through conformity to the requirements of the law. It is the attitude of death to self that makes it possible for the Holy Spirit to break the power of indwelling sin. It is the attitude of full surrender to the sphere of His complete control that makes it possible for the Holy Spirit to produce the positive fruits of righteousness in us (cf. Galatians 5:22).

In the preceding autobiographical section, especially after 7:14, the presence of the sin nature was the thing that hindered Paul, even as a Christian, from achieving spiritual victory. There was a constant conflict between the two natures — the new nature desiring that which is right, the old nature acclimated always toward that which is of sin. Paul expresses the same spiritual conflict in Galatians 5:17 — "For the flesh lusteth against the Spirit, and the Spirit against the flesh; for these are contrary the one to the other; that ye may not do the things that ye would."

Paul now addresses himself to this same controversy in verses 5-9a, but this time to show that the believer is heir to a new *motivation,* thus triumph in the conflict of the two natures is assured. The believer's assurance of victory in the conflict between the two natures is in verse 9a, "But ye are not in the flesh, but in the Spirit," i.e., when the believer is surrendered to the control of the indwelling Holy Spirit, He becomes the dominating force in the life. The result is that the power of the sin nature, which expresses itself in the flesh, is subjugated to this greater power. The believer thus lives under the dominion of this higher power, that of the indwelling Holy Spirit. This same truth Paul also expresses in verse 5 — "For they that are after the flesh mind the things of the flesh; but they that are after the Spirit the things of the Spirit." If it were not for the power of the Holy Spirit to restrain and dominate the sin nature, or the "mind of the flesh," then the believer would be once again drawn under its influence with the result that is enumerated in verses 6-8. But this is not the case because of the constant dominion of the "mind of the Spirit," resulting in life and peace.

Behind the new liberation and the new motivation that we have found in these verses, there is the more basic fact of the new *inhabitation* (verses 9-11), that is the residence of the Holy Spirit within the life of the believer. The conflict between the two natures, and the subsequent domination of the sin nature which Paul described in 7:14ff, is not due to an absence of the Holy Spirit. Every believer has the Holy Spirit residing within. This Paul affirms in verse 9b — "But if any man hath not the Spirit of Christ, he is none of his." The inevitable defeat in this conflict between the two natures is due to a condition of partial surrender to the Spirit's control, for He must have complete control in order to effect complete deliverance.

This great truth of the Spirit's abiding presence within each child of God means that even though "the body is dead because of sin," and thus devoid of any spiritual capacity, "the spirit is life because of righteousness" (verse 10). Paul returns again to the theme of Romans — the righteousness of God — as he draws to a close his discussion of victory over sin, in order to show that the righteousness of God has effected complete deliverance. It is one which looks not only to the past and the present, but which has prospect of final deliverance of the believer from the physical and spiritual dissolution of sin. This is the fullest expression of the righteousness of God.

In verses 10, 11 Paul moves to the climax of his discussion of the work of the Holy Spirit, for he has more than a present life of spiritual victory in mind here. Calvin felt that Paul's words should be restricted to the spiritual life; however this has been refuted by Hodge. Paul looks ahead to the believer's resurrection, which is the fullest extent of salvation; for we *have been saved* — justification; we are *being saved* — sanctification; and we are yet *to be saved* — glorification. It is the Holy Spirit who regenerates and who sanctifies, and who will also resurrect. Since the same Holy Spirit who raised up Christ from the dead dwells within us, He also guarantees our resurrection, for He "shall give life also to your mortal bodies through his Spirit that dwelleth in you" (verse 11).

The Scriptures attribute the resurrection of Christ to all members of the Trinity. It is at once the work of the Father (Acts 2:24, 32; Ephesians 1:17ff), the work of the Son (John

11:25; 10:17ff), and the work of the Holy Spirit (I Peter 3:18). Now the Holy Spirit is mentioned here as the specific Agent in our resurrection, yet there seems to be in Paul's mind the work of the entire Trinity in the believer's resurrection also. Note in verses 9-11 how Paul refers to the Holy Spirit in three different ways, each suggesting a different member of the Trinity: "Spirit of God" (verse 9a), "Spirit of Christ" (verse 9b), "Spirit of him that raised up Jesus," i.e., the Holy Spirit (verse 11).

A NEW REALIZATION OF SONSHIP

In the epistle of Romans Paul uses six great metaphors of salvation. They are justification, a metaphor of the law courts; reconciliation, a metaphor of friendship; redemption, a metaphor of slavery; propitiation, a metaphor of temple service; imputation, a metaphor of accounting; and adoption, a metaphor of family life. It is the last — the metaphor of adoption — that Paul uses as he now treats of a second great work of the Holy Spirit in the believer, namely, His work of assuring us that we are sons of God.

In verses 12-17a Paul points out three things that the Holy Spirit does with reference to our sonship. *First,* we are *made sons of God* by the Holy Spirit. This we find in verse 15 — "Ye received the Spirit of adoption whereby we cry, Abba, Father." The incoming presence of the Holy Spirit in a very definite sense constitutes us sons of God. One can become a member of an earthly family in only two ways: he may be born into a family, or he may be adopted. The Bible indicates that both measures are used to make us sons of God and members of God's family — and both of these operations are attributed to the Holy Spirit. We are constituted sons of God *practically* as we are *born* into His family by the regenerating work of the Holy Spirit. We are constituted sons of God *positionally,* i.e., before the law, as we are *adopted* into God's family. This too is a work of the Holy Spirit, as Paul tells us in these verses. This concept of adoption appears only in the writings of the apostle Paul. He alone uses the word "adoption." Paul was familiar with the Roman legal provision for adopting a person into a family not his own, and thus enabling one to enjoy all the benefits and privileges of the family as if he were an heir by natural birth. Paul was a Roman citizen. It seems natural then that he would make use of this metaphor to explain the work of the Holy Spirit in making us sons of God.

Being adopted as a child of God, the believer now utters the word "Father!" as a heartfelt reality. Paul says, "Abba, Father." Both words mean the same thing. The first one is Aramaic. It was often on the lips of Jesus, who spoke this language. The Old Testament speaks of God as the Father of Israel in a general sense, but the teaching of Jesus was radically new — this idea of God being the Father of each individual. The word "Abba" soon became a sacred word to the disciples of Christ because they had heard Him speak it so many times when He was here on earth. It passed into general usage in the Early Church, and so passed into the Greek language untranslated, and therefore into our English Bible untranslated. The sacred Hebrew words, "Amen" and "Hallelujah," did the same thing. Jesus taught this blessed new truth concerning the spiritual Fatherhood of God. But it is the Holy Spirit who makes it germane to the individual believer's experience through regeneration and adoption.

The key to understanding the blessings of adoption — for it has great practical value in our spiritual lives as well as positionally constituting us sons of God before the law — lies in noting the word "bondage." It appears in the context of Paul's use of "adoption" three out of the four times it occurs in his epistles. Adoption delivers the believer from physical bondage (Romans 8:21ff), from legal (spiritual) bondage (Galatians 4:5), and from bondage to fear, here in our current study. Thus all three vital areas of man's life are delivered from bondage, namely, the physical, the spiritual, and the mental, by the adopting work of the Holy Spirit as He introduces us into the glorious liberty of being sons of God.

There is a *second* thing that the Holy Spirit does with reference to our adoption. In verse 16 Paul points out that the Spirit not only makes us sons of God, but He also *makes us aware that we are sons of God.* "The Spirit himself beareth witness with our spirit that we are children of God." This is the beautiful doctrine of the witness of the Spirit, significant in the record of one of the greatest spiritual awakenings in modern history — the Evangelical Revival of the eighteenth century. John Wesley had much to say about the Spirit's witness to the experience of the new birth. It was *the* proof of salvation in those dramatic days. It is the Holy Spirit Himself that gives an assurance of salvation.

The King James says, "The Spirit itself." The grammatical gender of "Spirit" is neuter and it would seem that a neuter pronoun would best fit with it. However, A. T. Robertson says, "It is a grave mistake to use the neuter 'it' when referring to the Holy Spirit"[12] — the Greek sometimes uses the masculine with the neuter. Thus all modern translations follow the Revised Version in translating "the Spirit himself." The Holy Spirit is a Person, not an impersonal influence of power. Therefore, it is improper and irreverent for us to consider the Spirit as other than a Person. If we conceive of Him as an impersonal "it," or mere force, then our constant quest will be, "How can I get more of it?" But if we realize that He is a Person, then the reverse will be true — not "How can I get more of it?" but "How can He get more of me?"

What is meant by the "witness of the Spirit"?

We have already alluded to one feature that is a vital part of the Spirit's witness, i.e., it is a *personal* witness. "The Spirit himself" bears witness with our spirits that we are children of God. Scripture ascribes all the attributes of personality to the Holy Spirit — rationality (I Corinthians 2:11), volition (I Corinthians 12:11), and emotion (Romans 15:30). Thus there is contained in this personal witness a mental, emotional, and volitional contact between two rational personalities — that of the indwelling Holy Spirit and the believer, in whom He dwells. Our minds are informed by His personal presence. Our emotions are stirred by His personal presence, but not in an ecstatic sense. Our wills are moved by His personal presence. All of which is a proof that He dwells within and that we are therefore children of God.

There are objective proofs of salvation presented in the epistle of I John — 2:15, 29; 3:1, 9, 14; 5:2, 4, 13 — but the witness of the Spirit here in Romans is a very *subjective* thing. Paul says, "The Spirit himself beareth witness with our spirit"; hence the witness of the Spirit is not subject to external verification. However, John Wesley warned, "Let no man rest in a supposed witness of the Spirit apart from the fruit of the Spirit." The witness

[12] *Op. cit.*, p. 374.

of the Holy Spirit is an inward awareness produced by the indwelling Holy Spirit that we are children of God. Though we may not be able to adequately define this phenomena beyond that which we have already stated, every believer is keenly conscious of this inward assurance of salvation given by the Spirit, which is essentially a divine validation of the presence of the new birth. Most interpreters of Paul agree that he is making a point when he intentionally used "children of God" rather than "sons of God," in this verse. Son implies legal standing through adoption, while child of God suggests supernatural generation through the new birth. The witness of the Spirit is a subjective, inward testimony that the new birth has taken place.

The *third* important feature of adoption appears in verses 12-14. It is the power of the Spirit which enables us to *live as sons of God.* This reference is not limited to a concept of life beyond the grave, but includes living in the present a life of vital victory over sin. To be a child of God with no power to live up to all that this name inferred would be a mockery both to God and to the sinner. It would also suggest the absence of spiritual life, for Paul says in verse 13, "If ye live after the flesh, ye must die." Therefore there is provision through the indwelling Holy Spirit's presence, not only for the constitution and assurance of sonship, but also ample provision in His indwelling presence for enabling us to live a life of victory as children of God. Paul says in verse 14, "For as many as are led by the Spirit of God, these are sons of God." The leadership to which he refers is that which is suggested in verses 12, 13. In these verses we find a reiteration of that which Paul has already expounded in the preceding section, but with this valuable addition: verse 13 says, "If by the Spirit ye put to death the deeds of the body, ye shall live." Though he has inferred it throughout, for the first time Paul specifies the Holy Spirit as the direct Agent in mortifying the flesh. We are enabled to live as victorious sons of God because the Holy Spirit will accomplish this death to self for us when we reckon it to be so in faith. No wonder Paul says that we have a debt, not to live after the flesh, but after the Spirit (verse 12). It is not only the believer's privilege, but it also is his obligation to live a life of practical holiness, because God has provided all that is needed to make it possible through the Holy Spirit.

A New Philosophy of Suffering

In verse 17b Paul makes a statement that would seem almost self-contradictory to the Jew who might read these words. He affirms that we are children of God, joint heirs with Christ, and yet we are subject to suffering! The old Jewish philosophy posited suffering as the direct result of sin. It was experimental proof of unrighteousness. Now Paul completely reverses this conception. Though we are declared righteous through justification and made righteous through sanctification, yet we will suffer! How paradoxical! He follows these words with an apology in verse 18 for dealing with this subject in the light of its eternal insignificance, yet it is a necessary point in the discussion or righteousness in order to clarify the fact that suffering is not always the result of sin. When the righteous suffer, and they will, it is to be understood in *remedial* terms rather than in *punitive* ones. In addition, when suffering does come, we need to have an adequate understanding of God's providential purpose in permitting reverses to invade our lives.

Still relevant to the central theme of chapter 8 is the Holy Spirit's work in the life of the suffering believer. Paul points up three facts that will help us understand suffering and trials. There is a *theological* fact (verses 19-25); there is a *practical* fact (verses 26, 27); and there is a *philosophical* fact (verses 28-30).

In a certain sense the Jews were right in attributing suffering to sin, for behind the universal fact of suffering is the universal fact of sin and its consequent curse, which is the point at which suffering first issues in human experience. This is the *theological* presupposition behind all suffering (verses 19-25).

However, Paul now proclaims that the eminence of the Holy Spirit in human experience, and therefore in the universe itself, will guarantee ultimate deliverance. This cosmic reference is basic to our proper evaluation of the reason for, and the ultimate outcome of, suffering itself.

Paul has demonstrated two facts of personal experience thus far in Romans. The soul of man has deliverance from the curse of sin's penalty through justification. The life of the believer has deliverance from the curse of sin's power through sanctification. He now looks to the future and predicts a third deliverance, i.e., the deliverance of the physical creation from sin's abiding presence and curse. This is the ultimate potential of salvation, for which the creation itself now yearns (verse 19). This longing is not restricted to man, for Paul personifies the inanimate realm of nature and represents it as likewise longing for deliverance from sin's curse.

There is a very positive relationship between human sin and the physical world of created things. When man sinned, the inanimate world suffered along with man himself, for it was cursed as well as he in the primal fall (verse 20). But just as man's sin brought a curse to the creation, so man's ultimate deliverance will also result in the deliverance of the creation itself (verse 21).

The evidence for this lies in the eminence of the Holy Spirit in all things through His indwelling presence in the believer. He is the "firstfruits" (verse 23), which gives promise of ultimate, complete, and final deliverance of all things from sin's curse. This ultimate deliverance is latent in the experience of salvation itself and is therefore the foundation of our hope for cosmic salvation (verse 24ff).

Like the surge of an incoming tide, with each new revelation of the potentiality of salvation, Paul mounts higher and higher until he shows all the ramifications of the righteousness of God at work in redemption. The soul is saved, the life is saved, the body is saved, the race is saved, and now the whole creation enters into the experience of salvation as Paul shows the widest possible implications of this righteous act of God in redemption.

But until that time, we must remember that suffering is still a part of our experience, for ultimate deliverance has not come. It is yet only a hope, "for in hope we are saved" (verse 24). This hope which looks in anticipation to a future deliverance is an inseparable part of the very experience of salvation itself. As long as the universe still lies under the curse of sin, suffering is possible in every human experience, including that of the Christian. That is why Paul says, "For we know that the whole creation groaneth and travaileth in pain together until now" (verse 22). This theological fact is *a priori* in the whole problem, for it must be in the background of any adequate philosophy of suffering.

Prayer is a very difficult matter in the context of suffering, for at such times we do not know how to pray intelligently. This is due to the enigmatic and mysterious nature of suffering itself. Since we rarely understand why we suffer, we can rarely pray wisely in the midst of it. Should we pray for immediate and complete deliverance? Should we pray for patience to endure suffering? Numerous questions emerge during the dark hours of suffering which we cannot answer. Intelligent praying is as difficult as the suffering is mysterious, for one is commensurate with the other. What are we to do? Paul now presents a very *practical* fact of spiritual experience (verses 26, 27). Again the indwelling Holy Spirit comes to our aid to "help our infirmity" in prayer. Because "we know not how to pray as we ought," He makes "intercession for us according to the will of God." Ours may be an inarticulate sigh due to the mysterious nature of suffering, but He presents our prayer before the throne of God in spiritually articulate and acceptable form; hence guaranteeing that our prayer will be heard and answered.

There is but one perfect Man to ever appear on the stage of history, and of Him the Scriptures say, He was made "perfect through suffering" (Hebrews 2:10). The purpose of God for each believer is to transform him into the same image of that One perfect Man (verse 29). God has two ways of doing it. First, there is a more *formal* way, represented by the elective purposes of God in salvation. In verses 29, 30 the mind of Paul sweeps the entire expanse of salvation's experience, from foreknowledge in eternity past, to glorification in eternity future. He sees in election God's formal intention, through the various aspects of salvation, of transforming the sinner into the image of Christ. "For whom he foreknew, he also foreordained . . . and whom he foreordained, them he also called; and whom he called, them he also justified; and whom he justified, them he also glorified" (verses 29, 30).

But God has another way — an *experimental* way, which He couples with the more formal method of salvation in order to achieve this moral and spiritual transformation into the image of Christ. This experimental way is the way of suffering.

These two methods present us with the two sides of spiritual experience which we have had occasion to note several times before. Formally, by the elective purpose of God (verses 29, 30), we are transformed *positionally* into the image of Christ (note that Paul omits sanctification from the list, for it is of the *practical* rather than of the *positional*). Experimentally, by the providential means of suffering (verse 28), we are transformed *practically* into the image of Christ. Since it is axiomatic that we make greater spiritual advancement in the midst of suffering than in any other set of circumstances; therefore we are to see God's hand of permission in our suffering and realize "that to them that love God all things work together for good" (verse 28).

This verse may mean that God takes circumstances over which He has had no direct and decisive control and uses them for the believer's spiritual betterment. This is suggested by the marginal reading of the Revised Version. This position gives no credence to the permissive will of God, however, but puts the emphasis on the use God makes of circumstances in the believer's life after they have happened. If this is not the exact meaning of Paul, then we must take providential action one step further back and conceive of Paul's words, "All things work together for good," to mean that God allows nothing to touch the life of His child unless He directly wills and permits it. No matter what its source, if the yielded believer suffers it is because God designed this particular reverse, and His love permitted it under providential direction to come into the believer's life. With this philosophy of suffering, the Christian can meet reverses with the assurance that "all things *do* work together for good."

A NEW SONG OF TRIUMPH

We probably do Paul an injustice to examine these words in verses 31-39 too minutely, for they are poetry — a hymn of victory which forms a fitting climax not only to chapter 8, but also to what Paul has said in all the preceding chapters. In these verses he concludes his discussion thus far with a majestic affirmation of the security of the believer; for not only has the righteousness of God effected a *full* salvation, but it also guarantees a *permanent* one.

Christians have been divided on this issue of the security of the believer. Traditionally, the Calvinists have declared that the sovereignty of God will unconditionally keep man in a state of grace. The Arminians meanwhile have emphasized the freedom of man to remain a believer or to become an apostate. The Biblical view unites these two extremes of the divine and the human in a paradox. It teaches by its warning that it is *theoretically possible* for a person to fall away if he were left to his own way. However, it also teaches that it is *actually impossible* for a saved person to ever be lost again because of the purpose of God in election which guarantees the final outcome of spiritual experience. This, along with the ever constant love of God, is the theme of Paul's song of triumph.

There are certain real problems in the thesis that a saved person can lose his salvation, e.g., if a believer ever became lost after once being saved, then it would be impossible for him ever to be saved again, according to Hebrews 6:4-6. Also there is the question of what causes one to lose his salvation. The answer must be sin. But that answer only raises a more basic question — how much sin? The advocates of this position readily admit that sin will forfeit salvation, but they are at a loss to designate how much sin it takes to do it; just as the advocates of salvation by works are at a loss to say just how much good work it takes to achieve salvation. But logic forces the conclusion that if sin can do it, one sin is enough. To be consistent with this theology, one must die perfect in order to be assured of salvation. But are you perfect? If the answer is "no," then you are lost. If the answer is "yes," then you are a liar, according to I John 1:8. Since it is said of all liars, "their part shall be in the lake that burneth with fire and brimstone; which is the second death" (Revelation 21:8), then you are lost anyway. Hence there is a real dilemma which is insurmountable in this unscriptural thesis.

It is not the issue of human consistency that guarantees salvation, for in these verses Paul bases our assurance on the consistency of God's love. If God loved us *because* we loved Him, then He would love us *only so long* as we loved Him. Salvation would be contingent on the condition of our own heart. But God loved us as sinners and therefore saved us in that condition in consistency with His own love, not ours. It is the very consistency of the love of God that gives credence to the security of the believer. For if a Christian ever became lost, that would immediately indicate that God's love had been revoked. But this is impossible, because God must act consistently with Himself, and the Bible tells us "God is love" (I John 4:8). Thus salvation is as sure as the nature of God is consistent. The saved status of the believer can only change if God changes. Since immutability is a natural attribute of God, He will never change (Malachi 3:6). Therefore salvation can never be lost.

In Paul's hymn of triumph, victory is assured because of *what God has done for us* (verses 31-34a). That "God is for us" is guaranteed in that He "spared not his own son, but delivered him up for us all." Since all else must be inferior to God's first and greatest Gift, "how shall he not also with him freely give us all things?" (verse 32). Our security is inherent in the very Gift itself, for the greatness of the Giver infers the greatness of the Gift. The greatness of the Gift means that it must have *duration* as well as *content* in order to be truly great, for even a gift of great content would be of little value if it were perishable. However, the righteousness of God has provided an adequate salvation — one which is qualitative, and also quantitative. It is these two characteristics in conjunction that spell the greatness of the Gift.

Because of the qualitative and quantitative greatness of the Gift, shall anyone ever "lay anything to the charge of God's elect?" The answer is "No!" for if God is satisfied with what Christ has done for the sinner — and He must be, for He justifies the sinner on the basis of what Christ did — who is left to condemn? (verse 33).

The preceding looks to the past, showing that nothing can be laid to the charge of God's elect because of what God Himself has done for us. Paul now turns to the present, demonstrating that the greatness of our salvation is contingent on *what Christ is also doing for us now* (verse 34b). There is none "that condemneth" the believer because of the prevailing sufficiency of the work of Christ. *He died.* The death of Christ is an event in past history, but its effects are ever-present realities. John speaks of the present efficacy of the death of Christ when he says, "The blood of Jesus Christ his son cleanseth (Greek — *keeps on cleansing*) us from all sin" (I John 1:8). Here is another ground for security, viz., the continual efficacy of the Atonement. Many conceive of the blood of Christ as a cleansing agent for all past sin, but after salvation has taken place, it has no further promise for the believer and his sin. But this is not what John says, for he uses a word which means a "continual cleansing," hence the blood "keeps on cleansing" us from all sin — past, present, and future (for all of your sin was in the future when Christ died).

Let me illustrate. I have been in many revivals in the mountains of eastern Kentucky. Late in the afternoon the coal miners come out of the pits. Their faces are completely black, except for two spots of white — their eyes. Coal dust has blackened their faces, but the moment a speck of coal dust alighted in the eye, the tear ducts became operative and the speck was washed away, thus keeping the eyes white amid the blackness. That is what the constant cleansing power of the blood of Christ does for the soul of the believer. That is why a Christian can never be lost, for the moment he sins, the blood cleanses away the stain, because of the continual efficacy of its nature.

Christ arose. The Resurrection is God's authorization of the perfection of the work of Christ. The high priest under the Old Testament dispensation went in the Holy of Holies in the Tabernacle once a year to present an atonement for sin. But it had to be repeated annually because it was an imperfect and thus impermanent atonement. It got imperfect and therefore impermanent results. In contrast to this, we have the perfect and thus permanent work of Christ — guaranteed perfect and therefore permanent by His resurrection. That is why the writer of the book of Hebrews says, "For by one offering he hath perfected forever them that are sanctified" (10:14). Christ's offering was perfect, thus permanent, and it gets perfect thus permanent results. The result is perfect as the cause, and it is as permanent as the cause. They stand or fall together. If the result ever became imperfect by becoming impermanent (i.e., if a Christian ever lost his salvation) then the cause would also become imperfect and impermanent. That is why if a Christian ever lost his salvation he could never be saved a second time — unless Christ died a second time, for the imperfection of the result would immediately invalidate the perfection of the cause. This would also mean that if one Christian ever lost his salvation, then all believers would be lost because the work of Christ invalidated for one would then become invalid for all.

Christ ascended. There He is enthroned at the right hand of God where He "maketh intercession for us." He is another guarantee of the security of the believer. Some say Simon Peter lost his salvation. Did he? He momentarily denied that he had an acquaintance with Christ. However, in the midst of that experience — dark as it was — there was one star of hope that shone brightly in the blackness of that night. It was the memory of the words of Christ, spoken weeks before. Jesus had said, "Simon, Simon, behold Satan asked to have you, that he might sift you as wheat; but I made supplication for thee, that thy faith fail not" (Luke 22:31), and it did not, for Christ had prayed for him. If Simon lost his salvation, it would mean that the prayer of Christ went unanswered. If it did, that would in turn reflect on the person of Christ, for He prayed unconditionally — not conditionally as He did in Gethsemane. If Simon Peter lost his salvation, then the prayer of the Son of God went unanswered. That would mean that Jesus was either defective in character or in spiritual perception so that God could not honor His prayer. There emerges a dilemma: either a safe Simon Peter or a defective Saviour. And the security of the believer is posited on the same basis, for the ascended Saviour is now interceding for each of us, that our faith fail not, as He did while He was here on earth, the night before He died (John 17:15).

All of these pertinent implications are inherent in what Paul says about the present work of Christ in verse 34 — "It is Christ Jesus that died, yea rather, that was raised from the dead, who is at the right hand of God, who also maketh intercession for us."

The believer is also secure because of *what circumstances cannot do to him* (verses 35-39). Though faced with environmental perils — "tribulation, anguish, persecution, famine, nakedness, peril or sword" (verses 35, 36), he is secure. Prophesied perils are of no threat (verse 36). Here Paul quotes from Psalm 44:22 — "For thy sake we are killed all the day long; we are accounted as sheep for the slaughter." This is not merely an illustration that Paul picks from the Psalms. It is an argument, for "it is written" (literally, *it has been written and stands so now*). Here is parallel history, for the psalm pictures Israel as faithful to God, yet devastated by her enemies. Trials are not a sign that God has withdrawn His love. We suffer for His sake. Therefore, Paul relates this psalm to the present jeopardy of the believer. The mysterious perils of "death nor life" cannot harm. Neither the demonic perils of "angels, principalities or powers," nor the natural perils of "height, depth, nor any other created thing" (verse 38) can effect a separation between the redeemed soul and God.

The believer is "in all things more than conquerors through him that loved us" (verse 37) — not merely a negative security in the midst of these varied and numerous threats.

All this is ours because we are Christ's!

A Selected Bibliography

An exhaustive bibliography on the epistle to the Romans is at least worthy of a master's thesis and is therefore impossible to include in a popular exposition of this epistle. The bibliographical list which follows includes those works out of which background material has been drawn. A number of the older commentaries, including some Puritan works, have been included because of their rich suggestiveness. The systematic theologies are mentioned because of their clear instruction in the Pauline-Calvinistic doctrine of justification by faith alone. Volumes such as Mrs. Pearsall Smith's popular work on sanctification are helpful in understanding Romans 6 through 8 — since Keswick theology seems to have the most satisfying grasp of this portion of Scripture. The volume by Evan Hopkins mentioned in the bibliography is usually considered the standard expression of Keswick thought.

Alford, Henry. *The Greek New Testament.* Vol. II. London: Rivington, 1865.

Arnold, Albert N. and D. B. Ford. *Commentary on the Epistle to the Romans.* Philadelphia: American Baptist Publishing Society, 1889.

Barabas, Steven. *So Great Salvation.* London: Marshall, Morgan and Scott, 1952.

Barclay, William. *Ambassador for Christ.* Edinburgh: Church of Scotland Youth Committee, 1958.

———. *The Letter to the Romans* (The Daily Bible Study series). Philadelphia: Westminster, 1957.

———. *The Mind of St. Paul.* New York: Harper & Brothers, 1958.

———. *More New Testament Words.* London: Student Christian Movement, 1958.

———. *A New Testament Word Book.* London: Student Christian Movement, 1959.

Barnes, Albert. *Notes Explanatory and Practical on the Epistle to the Romans.* New York: Harper & Brothers, 1871.

Barnhouse, Donald Grey. *God's Wrath.* Wheaton, Ill.: Van Kampen Press, 1953.

———. *Man's Ruin.* Wheaton, Ill.: Van Kampen Press, 1952.

Barrett, C. Kingsley. *A Commentary on the Epistle to the Romans* (Harper's New Testament Commentaries series). New York: Harper & Brothers, 1957.

Barth, Karl. "Christ and Adam, Man and Humanity in Romans Five," in *Scottish Journal of Theological Occasional Papers, No. 5.* Trans. by T. A. Smail. Edinburgh: Oliver and Boyd, 1956.

———. *The Epistle to the Romans.* Trans. by Edwyn C. Hoskyns. London: Oxford University Press, 1957.

Bartlett, C. Norman. *Right in Romans.* Chicago: Moody Press, 1953.

Beet, Joseph Agar. *A Commentary on St. Paul's Epistle to the Romans.* London: Hodder & Stoughton, 1882.

———. *The New Life in Christ.* London: Hodder & Stoughton, 1896.

Bengel, John Albert. *Gnomen of the New Testament.* Trans. by James Bryce. Vol. III. Edinburgh: T. & T. Clark, 1895.

Berkhof, Louis. *Systematic Theology.* London: Banner of Truth, 1959.

Bickersteth, Edward. *A Practical and Explanatory Commentary on the New Testament.* Vol. III. London: Virtue, n.d.

Binning, Hugh. *Works.* Glasgow: Fullarton, 1842.

Bloomfield, S. T. *The Greek New Testament.* London: Longmans, Green & Co., 1874.

Brown, David. *The Epistle to the Romans.* Edinburgh: T. & T. Clark, 1950.

Brunner, Emil. *The Christian Doctrine of Creation and Redemption (Dogmatics,* Vol. II). Trans. by Olive Wyon. London: Lutterworth Press, 1952.

———. *The Letter to the Romans.* Trans. by H. A. Kennedy. London: Lutterworth Press, 1959.

Burkitt, W. *Expository Notes With Practical Observations on the New Testament.* London: Kelley, 1819.

Burns, James. *Revivals, Their Laws and Leaders.* London: Hodder & Stoughton, 1909.

Burrows, W. *A Homiletical Commentary on the Epistle of St. Paul the Apostle to the Romans (The Preacher's Homiletical Commentary* series). New York: Funk & Wagnalls, 1896.

Buttrick, George, ed. *The Interpreter's Bible.* Vol. IX. New York: Abingdon-Cokesbury Press, 1954.

Calvin, John. *Commentary Upon the Epistle of St. Paul to the Romans* (edition from Rosdell's translation by Henry Beveridge). Edinburgh: Calvin Translation Society, 1844.

Carroll, B. H. *An Interpretation of the English Bible.* Vol. X. Nashville: Broadman Press, 1942.

Chrysostomus, Joannes. *The Homilies on the Epistle of St. Paul the Apostle to the Romans.* Trans. by J. Parker. Oxford: Rivington, 1841.

Clark, Adam. *The Holy Bible.* Vol. IV. Cincinnati: Applegate, 1856.

Clarke, W. K. Lowther. *Concise Bible Commentary.* London: SPAC, 1952.

Coates, C. A. *An Outline of the Epistle to the Romans.* London: Stow Hill Bible & Tract Depot, n.d.

Comper, James. *The Biblical Museum.* Vol. III. London: Stock, 1880.

Conner, Walter T. *The Gospel of Redemption.* Nashville: Broadman, 1945.

Cook, F. C., ed. *The Holy Bible*. Vol. III. London: Murray, 1893.

Davidson, A. B. *The Theology of the Old Testament*. Edinburgh: T. & T. Clark, 1949.

Davidson, F., ed. *The New Bible Commentary*. London: Inter-Varsity, 1953.

Davies, G. H., Alan Richardson, and C. L. Wallis. *The Twentieth Century Bible Commentary*. New York: Harper & Brothers, 1955.

Deissmann, Adolph. *Paul — a Study in Social and Religious History*. New York: Harper & Brothers, 1957.

Denney, James. *St. Paul's Epistle to the Romans* (The Expositor's Greek Testament series). Vol. II. New York: Dodd, Mead & Co., 1910.

Dodd, C. H. *The Epistle of Paul to the Romans* (Moffatt New Testament Commentary series). London: Hodder & Stoughton, 1949.

Dykes, J. Oswald. *The Gospel According to St. Paul*. London: Nisbet, n.d.

Eckardt, A. Roy. *The Surge of Piety in America*. New York: Association Press, 1958.

Eiselen, F. C. *The Minor Prophets*. New York: Eaton & Mains, 1907.

———, Edwin Lewis, and David Downey, eds. *The Abingdon Bible Commentary*. Nashville: Abingdon-Cokesbury, 1929.

Excell, Joseph S. *Romans* (The Biblical Illustrator series). 2 vols. London: Griffiths, 1908.

Figgis, J. B. *Keswick From Within*. London: Marshall, n.d.

Forbes, John. *Analytical Commentary on the Epistle to the Romans*. Edinburgh: T. & T. Clark, 1868.

Forrester, E. J. *A Righteousness of God for Unrighteous Man*. Nashville: Sunday School Board of the Southern Baptist Convention, 1926.

Forsyth, P. T. *The Work of Christ*. London: Hodder & Stoughton, n.d.

Garvie, Alfred E. *Romans* (The Century Bible series). Edinburgh: Jack, 1901.

Gaustad, Edwin Scott. *The Great Awakening in New England*. New York: Harper & Brothers, 1957.

Gill, John. *An Exposition of the New Testament*. Vol. II. London: Matthews & Leigh, 1809.

Godet, F. *Commentary on the Epistle to the Romans*. Grand Rapids: Zondervan Publishing House, 1956.

Gordon, A. J. *The Ministry of the Spirit*. Philadelphia: The Judson Press, 1949.

———. *The Two-Fold Life*. New York: Revell, 1883.

Gore, Charles. *St. Paul's Epistle to the Romans*. 2 vols. London: Murray, 1900.

Grant, Fredrick C. *An Introduction to New Testament Thought*. Nashville: Abingdon, 1950.

Gray, James. *Synthetic Bible Studies*. New York: Fleming H. Revell, 1906.

Gray, James C., and George M. Adams. *The Biblical Encyclopedia*. Vol. V. Cleveland: Barton, 1903.

Griffith, Gwilym Oswald. *St. Paul's Gospel to the Romans*. Oxford: Blackwell, 1949.

Grubs, Isaiah Boone. *An Exegetical and Analytical Commentary on Paul's Epistle to the Romans*. Cincinnati: 1913.

Haldane, Robert. *Exposition of the Epistle to the Romans*. Edinburgh: Oliphant, 1874.

Halley, Henry H. *Bible Handbook*. Grand Rapids: Zondervan Publishing House, 1959.

Hanna, William. *Selected Works of Thomas Chalmers, D.D., LL.D.* Vols. I-II. Edinburgh: Constable, 1856.

Harshman, Samuel R. *A Commentary, Doctrinal and Practical, on the Epistle of Paul the Apostle to the Romans*. Akron: Warner, 1904.

Hastings, James. *Dictionary of the Apostolic Church*. 2 vols. New York: Charles Scribner's Sons, 1916.

Hawker, Robert. *The Poor Man's Commentary on the New Testament*. Vol. II. London: Neely & Jones, 1815.

Heisch, J. *Reflections Exegetical and Experimental on St. Paul's Epistle to the Romans*. London: Nisbet, 1891.

Henry, Carl F., ed. *The Biblical Expositor*. Philadelphia: A. J. Holman Co., 1960.

Henry, Matthew. *Commentary on the Whole Bible*. Grand Rapids: Zondervan Publishing House, 1960.

Hodge, Charles. *Commentary on the Epistle to the Romans*. Unabridged edition from the 1886 revision. Grand Rapids: Eerdmans Publishing Co., 1955.

————. *Commentary on the Epistle to the Romans*. Abridged edition by the author. Philadelphia: Perkins, 1836.

Hoffman, Fred W. *Revival Times in America*. Boston: W. A. Wilde Co., 1956.

Hopkins, Evan. *The Law of Liberty in the Spiritual Life*. London: Marshall, Morgan and Scott, 1952.

Hunter, A. M. *The Epistle to the Romans* (Torch Bible Commentary series). London: Student Christian Movement, 1955.

Ironside, H. A. *Lectures on the Epistle to the Romans*. New York: Loizeaux Brothers, 1944.

Johnson, Henry. *Stories of Great Revivals*. London: Religious Trust Society, 1906.

Jowett, Benjamin. *The Epistle of St. Paul to the Thessalonians, Galatians, Romans*. Vol. II. London: Murray, 1859.

Keil, C. F., and Franz Delitzsch. *Biblical Commentary on the Old Testament — the Twelve Minor Prophets*. Vol. II. Trans. by James Martin. Grand Rapids: Wm. B. Eerdmans Publishing Co., 1949.

Knox, John. *Life in Christ Jesus*. Greenwich, Conn.: Seabury, 1961.

Lange, J. P. and F. R. Fay. *The Epistle of Paul to the Romans*. Vol. V. Trans. by J. F. Hurst. New York: Charles Scribner's Sons, 1872.

Lard, Moses. *Commentary on Paul's Letter to Romans*. Lexington, Ky.: Transylvania Printing Co., 1875.

Leenhardt, Franz. *The Epistle to the Romans.* London: Lutterworth Press, 1961.

Lenski, R. C. H. *The Interpretation of St. Paul's Epistle to the Romans.* Columbus: Wartburg Press, 1945.

Liddon, H. P. *Explanatory Analysis of St. Paul's Epistle to the Romans.* London: Longmans, Green and Co., 1893.

Livermore, A. A. *The Epistle of Paul to the Romans.* Boston: Crosby, Nichols, 1854.

Luther, Martin. *Commentary on the Epistle to the Romans.* Trans. by J. Theodore Mueller. Grand Rapids: Zondervan Publishing House, 1956.

Luthi, Walter. *The Letter to the Romans.* Trans. by Kurt Schoenenberger. Richmond, Va.: John Knox Press, 1961.

Macduff, John R. *St. Paul's Song of Songs.* London: Nisbet, 1891.

Machen, J. Gresham. *The Origin of Paul's Religion.* New York: The Macmillan Co., 1921.

Meyer, F. B. *The Christ-life for the Self-life.* Chicago: Moody Press, 1897.

Meyer, Heinrich August Wilhelm. *Critical and Exegetical Handbook to the Epistle to the Romans.* 2 vols. Trans. by William P. Dickson. Edinburgh: T. & T. Clark, 1873.

Moffatt, James. *An Introduction to the Literature of the New Testament.* Edinburgh: T. & T. Clark, 1949.

Morgan, G. Campbell. *Living Messages of the Books of the Bible.* Vol. II. New York: Fleming H. Revell, 1912.

———. *The Epistle of Paul the Apostle to the Romans.* London: Hodder & Stoughton, 1909.

Moule, Handley C. G. *The Epistle of St. Paul to the Romans (The Expositor's Bible* series). New York: Armstrong, 1903.

———. *The Epistle of Paul the Apostle to the Romans. (Cambridge Bible for Schools and Colleges* series). Cambridge: Cambridge University Press, 1952.

Mullins, E. Y. *The Christian Religion in Its Doctrinal Expression.* Philadelphia: The Judson Press, 1949.

———. *Why Is Christianity True?* Philadelphia: The Judson Press, 1905.

Murray, John. *The Epistle to the Romans (The New International Commentary* series). Grand Rapids: Wm. B. Eerdmans Publishing Co., 1959.

———. *The Imputation of Adam's Sin.* Grand Rapids: Wm. B. Eerdmans Publishing Co., 1959.

Nygren, Anders. *Commentary on Romans.* Trans. by Carl C. Rasmussen. Philadelphia: Muhlenberg Press, 1949.

Ockenga, Harold J. *Every One That Believeth.* New York: Fleming H. Revell, 1942.

Orr, James. *The Progress of Dogma.* New York: Armstrong, 1901.

———. *The Second Evangelical Awakening in America.* London: Marshall, Morgan & Scott, 1952.

Parker, Joseph. *The People's Bible.* Vol. XXIV. London: Hazell, Watson & Viney, 1907.

Parry, R. St. John. *The Epistle of Paul the Apostle to the Romans (Cambridge Greek Testament for Schools and Colleges* series). Cambridge: Cambridge University Press, 1912.

Patrick, et al. *Critical Commentary and Paraphrase of the Old and New Testament.* London: Tegg, 1842.

Peake, Arthur. *A Commentary on the Bible.* New York: Nelson, n.d.

Philippi, Fredrich Adolph. *Commentary on St. Paul's Epistle to the Romans.* 2 vols. Trans. by J. S. Banks. Edinburgh: T. & T. Clark, 1878.

Phillips, J. B. *Letters to Young Churches.* London: Bles, 1947.

Pool, Matthew. *Annotations Upon the Holy Bible.* London: Nisbet, 1880.

Pusey, E. B. *The Minor Prophets.* Vol. II. Grand Rapids: Baker Book House, 1950.

Quimby, Chester W. *Paul for Everyone.* New York: The Macmillan Co., 1944.

Rainsford, Marcus. *Lectures on Romans V.* London: Hoby, n.d.

———. *Lectures on Romans VI.* London: Hoby, n.d.

———. *Lectures on Romans VII.* London: Hoby, n.d.

———. *No Condemnation — No Separation, Lectures on Romans VIII.* London: Hodder & Stoughton, 1885.

Ripley, Henry Jones. *The Epistle of the Apostle Paul to the Romans.* Boston: Gould & Lincoln, 1857.

Robertson, A. T. *Epochs in the Life of Paul.* New York: Charles Scribner's Sons, 1909.

———. *New Testament Interpretation.* Stenographic Lectures taken by Davidson. Louisville, 1921.

———. *Word Pictures in the New Testament.* Vol. VI. Nashville: Broadman, 1931.

Robinson, Thomas. *A Suggestive Commentary on St. Paul's Epistle to the Romans.* 2 vols. London: Dickinson, 1878.

Sanday, William. *The Epistle to the Romans (Layman's Handy Commentary* series, C. J. Ellicott, ed.). Grand Rapids: Zondervan Publishing House, 1957.

———, and Arthur Headlam. *The Epistle to the Romans (The International Critical Commentary* series.) Edinburgh: T. & T. Clark, 1950.

Scott, E. F. *The Literature of the New Testament.* New York: Columbia University Press, 1946.

———. *Paul's Epistle to the Romans.* New York: Student Christian Movement, 1947.

Scott, Thomas. *The Holy Bible.* Vol. VI. London: Seeley, 1823.

Shepherd, C. P. *The Argument of St. Paul's Epistle to the Christians in Rome.* London: Bell & Daldy, 1862.

Simon, J. S. *The Revival of Religion in England in the Eighteenth Century.* London: Kelley, n.d.

Smith, David. *The Life and Letters of St. Paul*. New York: Harper & Brothers, n.d.

Smith, Hannah W. *The Christian's Secret of a Happy Life*. London: Nisbet, 1904.

Smith, Timothy L. *Revivalism and Social Reform*. Nashville: Abingdon, 1957.

Spence, H. D., and Joseph S. Excell, eds. *Romans (The Pulpit Commentary* series). London: Paul, Trench & Trubner, 1890.

Stevens, G. B. *The Christian Doctrine of Salvation*. Edinburgh: T. & T. Clark, 1930.

———. *The Theology of the New Testament*. Edinburgh: T. & T. Clark, 1931.

Stewart, James S. *A Man in Christ*. New York: Harper & Brothers, n.d.

Strong, A. H. *Systematic Theology*. Vol. III. Philadelphia: The Judson Press, 1909.

Stuart, Moses. *A Commentary on the Epistle to the Romans*. London: Tegg, 1838.

Sutcliffe, Joseph. *A Commentary on the Old and New Testament*. Vol. II. London: Mason, 1838.

Swete, William Warren. *Religion in Colonial America*. New York: Charles Scribner's Sons, 1953.

Taylor, Vincent. *The Epistle to the Romans (Epworth Preacher's Commentaries* series). London: Epworth, 1955.

Tholuck, Fredrick August Gottreu. *Exposition of St. Paul's Epistle to the Romans*. Trans. by Robert Menzies. Philadelphia: Sorin & Ball, 1844.

Thomas, W. H. Griffith. *Romans (The Devotional Commentary* series). 3 vols. London: Religious Tract Society, n.d.

Throckmorton, Burton H. *Romans for the Layman*. Philadelphia: Westminster, 1961.

Torrey, R. A. *Real Salvation*. New York: Fleming H. Revell, 1905.

Trapp, John. *A Commentary on the New Testament*. Reprint from 1865 edition. Grand Rapids: Zondervan Publishing House, 1958.

Trench, Richard. *Synonyms of the New Testament*. London: The Macmillan Co., 1876.

Tyson, William. *Expository Lectures on the Epistle of Paul the Apostle to the Romans*. London: Wesleyan, 1882.

Vaughan, C. J. *St. Paul's Epistle to the Romans*. London: The Macmillan Co., 1880.

Vincent, Marvin R. *Word Studies in the New Testament*. Vol. III. Grand Rapids: Eerdmans Publishing Co., 1946.

Vine, W. E. *A Comprehensive Dictionary of the Original Greek Words With Their Precise Meanings for English Readers*. 4 vols. London: Oliphants, 1946.

Ward, Wayne E. "The Theology of the Roman Epistle," in Duke K. McCall, ed., *Review and Expositor*. Vol. LIV, Number 1 (January, 1957). Louisville: Southern Baptist Theological Seminary, 1957.

Wardlaw, Ralph. *Lectures on the Epistle to the Romans.* 2 vols. Edinburgh: Fullarton, 1869.

Warfield, B. B. *The Plan of Salvation.* Grand Rapids: Eerdmans Publishing Co., 1955.

Weber, Otto. *The Ground Plan of the Bible.* Trans. by Harold Knight. Philadelphia: Westminster Press, 1959.

Weisberger Bernard A. *They Gathered at the River.* Boston: Little, Brown & Co., 1958.

Weiss, Bernhard. *A Commentary on the New Testament.* Trans. by Schodde and Wilson. Vol. III. New York: Funk & Wagnalls, 1906.

Williams, Charles B. *A Commentary on the Pauline Epistles.* Chicago: Moody Press, 1953.

Winslow, Octavius. *No Condemnation in Christ Jesus — Romans Eight.* London: Farquhar Shaw, 1853.

Woods, Edward S. *The Epistle to the Romans.* New York: Doubleday, Doran, n.d.

Wuest, Kenneth. *Romans in the Greek New Testament.* Grand Rapids: Eerdmans Publishing Co., 1956.